# Praying
## WITH A Pen

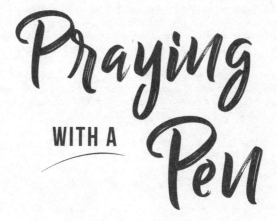

# Praying
## WITH A Pen

*The Girlfriends' Guide
to Stress-Free
Prayer Journaling*

**MARY BETH WEISENBURGER**

**BEACON PUBLISHING**
North Palm Beach, Florida

Unless otherwise noted, Scripture passages have been taken from the
*Revised Standard Version, Catholic Edition*. Copyright © 1946, 1952, 1971 by
the Division of Christian Education of the National Council of Churches
of Christ in the USA. Used by permission. All rights reserved.

Quotes are taken from the English translation of the *Catechism of the
Catholic Church* for the United States of America (indicated as *CCC*), 2nd
edition. Copyright © 1997 by United States Catholic Conference—Libreria
Editrice Vaticana.

Design by Ashley Wirfel

ISBN: 978-1-929266-48-7 (softcover)
ISBN: 978-1-929266-49-4 (e-book)

Library of Congress Cataloging-in-Publication Data
Names: Weisenburger, Mary Beth, author.
Title: Praying with a pen : the girlfriends' guide to stress-free prayer
journaling / Mary Beth Weisenburger.
Description: North Palm Beach, Florida : Beacon Publishing, [2017]
Identifiers: LCCN 2017027695 | ISBN 9781929266487 (softcover) |
ISBN 9781929266494 (e-book)
Subjects: LCSH: Prayer—Catholic Church. | Spiritual journals. |
Spiritual life—Catholic Church.
Classification: LCC BV210.3 .W44 2017 | DDC
248.4/6—dc23

Dynamic Catholic® and Be Bold. Be Catholic.® and The Best Version of
Yourself® are registered trademarks of The Dynamic Catholic Institute.

For more information on this title or other books and CDs available
through the Dynamic Catholic Book Program,
please visit www.DynamicCatholic.com.

The Dynamic Catholic Institute
5081 Olympic Blvd • Erlanger • Kentucky • 41018
Phone: 1–859–980–7900
Email: info@DynamicCatholic.com

First printing, August 2017

Printed in the United States of America

# DEDICATION

*To my witty and wonderful husband, Steve,
and our never-a-dull-moment children, Curtis and Erin—
I love you forever.*

# Table of Contents

**INTRODUCTION:** I Didn't See That Coming    1

**ONE:** Jumping Your Hurdles    7

**TWO:** Be Quiet!    15

**THREE:** A Simple Start—The Four P's of Praying with a Pen    27

**FOUR:** Do It Like This (If You Want to)    39

**FIVE:** Open the Catholic Treasure Chest    53

**SIX:** A Spiritual Shopping Spree    65

**SEVEN:** Tips, Tricks, Boosts, and Hacks    83

**EIGHT:** Those Tiny (and Not So Tiny) Revelations    95

**NINE:** Good Bye, Catholic Couch Potato    107

**TEN:** Real Rest    115

**APPENDIX:** Forty Prayer Journal Questions/Prompts/
Conversation Starters    125

**ENDNOTES**    127

# Introduction

## I DIDN'T SEE THAT COMING

Greetings, Catholic girlfriend!

Do you remember receiving special stickers for memorizing your Catholic prayers way back when? I vividly recall standing at my religion teacher's desk at St. Michael Elementary School to recite a prayer so she could reward me with a coveted gold star sticker. I didn't care that the glue on the back of the star left a disgusting taste in my mouth—this was progress, people! That star was going right below the other stars on my blue mimeographed prayer card. My memorization efforts eventually led up to the triumphant moment when I earned a supersize, shiny silver praying-hands sticker for reciting the final assignment: the Apostles' Creed. Victory! My goal was met; my prayer formation was complete. Or so I thought . . .

Fast forward twenty years to when I found myself firmly ensconced in a Protestant church with my Protestant husband. I had rather nonchalantly abandoned my Catholic upbringing after I got married, and I soon learned that my memorized Catholic prayers were not one bit helpful in this new setting. Here, Scripture verses were to be memorized, but prayer was to be straight from my heart to Jesus' ears. *What?* I thought. *A different prayer every time I sat down for a meal? A different prayer at bedtime? A different prayer when I discovered my two-year-old flushed his underwear down the toilet while I was trying to rock his colicky baby sister?* It was more than a little intimidating. *What do I say? How do I start? Will people laugh at my apprehension and my lack of instinct when talking to Jesus one-on-one? Or worse yet, will my stumblings and stutterings make Jesus want to slap his own forehead in disbelief?* (I'm sure I have caused him to do this, if only in my imagination, on many other occasions throughout my life.)

I was intrigued by the idea of informal, personal prayer, but oh-so-inexperienced at it. I needed a way to practice this new notion. That's when I began the habit of prayer journaling, even though that's not what I called it at the time. My early writings were known as Morning Pages, based on a technique taught by Julia Cameron in her popular book for aspiring writers, *The Artist's Way*.[1] Back then, I was hoping to become a columnist and author, so it made sense for me to practice both my writing and my praying at the same time (I'm a two-birds-with-one-stone kind of gal). As soon as possible after I woke up every morning, I sat in a comfy corner chair with a hot drink, a good pen, and a ninety-nine-cent notebook. And I started writing— three pages every day as recommended. It was mostly random ramblings with a bit of prayer time added at the end. Day after day, week after week, month after month.

And then, slowly but surely, amazing things began to happen. Amazing little things and amazing big things too. Seriously, I mean eye-opening, jaw-dropping, life-altering things. Things. I. Did. Not. See. Coming.

As I began to write down my thoughts about my little corner of the world and pray about my hopes and dreams, I began to realize something. Oh, I was getting more comfortable conversing with God one-on-one, sure. And I did eventually become a columnist, and then an author. But more than that, way more than that, I discovered something very important: When I sat down to scribble on lined paper every morning, with groggy eyes and an even groggier brain, *I was writing to God.*

And, girlfriend . . . *he was writing back to me.*

Right there in that cheap notebook—Father, Son, Holy Spirit—they all "wrote" back to me.

Don't be alarmed—I didn't hear actual voices. But I did "hear" quiet, gentle answers through the writing process. When I asked questions, the answers somehow flowed from my heart down my arm, through the ink, and onto the paper. I saw them come to life on the page. My questions and prayers and wonderings were being addressed. Not always as I wanted, of course. And definitely not always right away. But eventually I could see positive changes in my life, and I could clearly connect those outcomes to the graces I received through my prayer journaling habit. And bonus—over the course of my prayer journaling experience, my anxieties lessened, my faith blossomed, and my nagging doubts were overpowered by some holy confidence I had never possessed before. I found a new kind of peace through prayer journaling.

And something else pretty wild happened: My hard, independent, self-sufficient heart began to, incredibly, soften. Just a smidge at first, but enough to let the Holy Spirit slip in and start some heavy-duty housecleaning. Jesus was working on me. *Me!* He was helping me, prodding me, talking to me through the pages of my prayer journal. He was calling me, like one of his lost sheep. And, miracle of all grand miracles, I returned home to the Catholic Church in February 2013, largely because of my prayer journaling experience.

I told you it was amazing! All that from a pen and a notebook and a simple desire to draw nearer to an arms-wide-open God. It's been nothing short of an adventure. St. John Paul II said it: "Life with Christ is a wonderful adventure."[2]

This experience is not reserved for me. You are about to embark on a marvelous journey too, sister—one designed just for you. Think for a second: Why did you pick up this book? What's your particular spiritual concern or challenge right now? Do you struggle with prayer like me? Do you need a practical way to focus your attention on God in the midst of your hyper-scheduled life? Are you unsure if God is even working in your life at all? Stick with me, my friend. Praying with a pen can take your prayer life to a new level if you give it a chance. And even if you feel somewhat satisfied with your spiritual life at the moment, prayer journaling can open the doors to even more graces. God can and will take the good and make it even better!

Trust me—you don't have to be a writer to join in this adventure. You don't have to be a theologian. You don't even have to feel confident in your faith. You only need to have an open, willing heart and a desire to grow closer to Jesus.

That's it. I promise.

Find a quiet spot to write, and he will meet you there. In fact, he's already there, waiting for you with a big smile on his face. He has been calling you and is delighted that you want to spend time with him.

Let's get this adventure started, shall we? Let's go pray with a pen.

Your new prayer journaling partner,
Mary Beth

P.S. You may be tickled to note that when I returned to the Catholic faith, all those prayers I memorized in third grade came rushing back to me. I think that calls for one more gold star, don't you?

# One

## JUMPING YOUR HURDLES

*Draw near to God, and he will draw near to you.*
*James 4:8*

I get it. You are one busy woman. You have a million and two things to do. So many priorities. So many responsibilities. Why in the world would you commit to something like prayer journaling that takes such precious time out of your hectic day?

Well, first and foremost, because God wants you to! He is your Creator and you are his beloved daughter. That's right, *beloved*. Dearly loved. Overwhelmingly loved. He knows you better than anyone else does. He loves you more than anyone else does. And he wants you to spend time with him over anything else. He wants to draw you near and pull you close and open up your heart to a full relationship with him. And guess what? As the above verse promises, if you draw near to him, a remarkable thing happens: He will draw near to you. The God of the Universe will draw near to *you*. Little 'ole you, in your small town or your big city or your cabin in the mountains. He wants to connect with you. He wants to have a conversation with you. Prayer journaling is one easy way to let him do that every day; it puts you in a position to be found by your Creator! It will help you pray to him like never before and can deepen your relationship with him in surprising and rewarding ways.

Another reason to give prayer journaling a chance (if you need another reason!) is based on something my Grandma Eleanor taught me: *Work your spiritual muscles!* Grandma got up at dawn and was in perpetual motion all day long. She made breads and cakes and award-winning pies from scratch. She sewed clothes for her nine children. She knew every home remedy there was to know when a doctor was nearly impossible to find. And she worked the fields right alongside her husband. She was no lightweight. She lived to be ninety-six years old!

Grandma knew how to stay healthy physically and spiritually. She believed a person needed to work his or her physical muscles every day in order to live a long life, and she knew a good spiritual muscle workout was also a necessity. Daily prayer was required, and the beads of her rosary were well-worn by the time I inherited it. Smart woman. I don't recall if she kept a prayer journal, but I'm sure she would consider it a worthwhile tool in the spiritual fitness regimen. It just makes old-fashioned common sense: When we exercise our spiritual muscles daily, there's less chance of getting spiritually sick. Daily prayer journaling is like taking spiritual vitamins. (Or—for those of us old enough to understand this reference—it's like eating our spiritual Wheaties!)

I could rattle off dozens more reasons to take up prayer journaling. Here are several:

- You will face the day's challenges more confidently.
- You will feel refreshed.

- You will develop a greater sense of peace, joy, contentment, gratitude, calm.
- You will discover a deeper understanding of yourself and your faith.
- You will see God's hand in your life more clearly.
- You will gain more clarity and find it easier to make life decisions.

The list goes on. Researchers have long touted the benefits of journaling in general. Journaling clarifies your thoughts and feelings, reduces stress, and helps you solve problems. And to top it off, journaling can also strengthen your immune cells![3] There's clearly something about writing down your thoughts and petitions and prayers in a quiet setting that adds a measure of intensity and focus and gets your whole being—mind, body, and spirit—involved. Aside from going to Mass and receiving the sacraments, prayer journaling could be more fruitful than almost any practice you have implemented in your spiritual life!

Debbie Guardino, a speaker, writer, and blogger, is also a fan of the prayer journaling habit. She always recommends prayer journaling whenever she speaks on the topic of prayer. She calls it a "faith builder and a trust builder" and says, "If you want to see growth, this is a tremendous way to do it. Prayer journaling keeps my prayer life fresh. It can benefit anyone!"[4]

## STILL HAVE RESERVATIONS?
Let's get all those remaining objections out on the table right now, OK? We'll just grab a squirt gun and fire away at them.

*This is just too weird.* This could be something really foreign to you, I know. Many Catholics, especially those of us who are—*cough, cough*—middle-aged, are unfamiliar with this notion of talking to God beyond using the prayers we were taught as children. During the twenty-plus years I spent away from the Catholic Church, years when I attended a Protestant church with my husband and children, I learned many wonderful things from my Christian brothers and sisters. One of those blessings was the importance of unscripted conversation with Jesus. They made it all so . . . simple. Uncomplicated. Personal. I had missed that lesson in my Catholic upbringing, and unfortunately, many from my era did too. Younger Catholics may find it just as challenging. Let's face it: In a world that increasingly seems to barely recognize God at all, informal prayer can be challenging no matter what age we are. But through prayer journaling, informal converation with Jesus eventually became more comfortable for me, and it will become more comfortable for you as well.

*I'm afraid I'm going to mess it up somehow.* You are God's beloved child. Remember? *Beloved!* This is your time to just sit back and be his daughter while you journal. If you stumble and fall and stop journaling for a while, forgive yourself (God does!) and get back to it as soon as you can. No one is keeping track or tallying the score. Just the fact that you're reading this book and have a desire to talk more to God already makes him happy. He is delighted by your effort and intention. You can't mess it up.

*I just don't have time—I can barely manage to brush my teeth every day.* I hear ya. I recall when my first child was born and I was on maternity leave. My husband would return home from work at the end of the day and find me still in my bathrobe—I had two college degrees, but I couldn't find a way to take a shower while I was caring for my newborn. Happily (for all of us), I settled into a routine and managed to figure out how to fit in appropriate personal hygiene. Here's the ugly truth, girlfriend: For most of us, it's all about priorities. And taking that first intentional step. And maybe setting your alarm a few minutes earlier, or giving up some social media time, or asking for a little help in the mornings if needed. In later chapters of this book, we'll go over some tips and tricks to finding the time to spend with Jesus.

*I hate to write; I just hate it.* Don't hyperventilate over this one, my friend. Prayer journaling is a low-stress form of writing—no brown paper bags will be needed to keep you from panicking. Your writing is never graded, it doesn't require those tedious footnotes that made us all despise writing term papers, and it doesn't have to follow any particular style. It's just you and the pen and the paper and whatever you want to write, however you want to write it. You don't even have to write in sentences! Now, that's not something your high school English teacher would approve of, but believe me, God doesn't care about spelling or grammar or sentence structure or the legibility of your handwriting. Neither should you. And breathe even easier, my friend: No artistic talent is necessary in prayer journaling. All those new, trendy journals that promote drawings and decorations and multicolor pens and pencils are not the point here. It says "stress-free" in this book's subtitle, right? We're going to keep it simple. It's about heart-to-heart communication with God, not creating a work of art or writing a best-selling novel.

*I feel funny keeping a diary at my age.* Does the idea of prayer journaling bring back embarrassing memories of your annoying brother finding your diary and telling the world that you had a crush on that cute boy in your class? (This may or may not have happened to me.) Well, here's the good news: Prayer journaling is not the same as keeping a diary. Oh sure, there will be times when you will need to review your day, discuss a problem with Jesus, or try to work through a life event. And you will want to keep your journal private as you would a diary. But prayer journaling is not a litany of your daily actions, the hilarious thing your cat did, or your ongoing diet challenges (although it's OK to pray that you will stick to your healthy eating plan— speaking from experience here!). Prayer journaling is *prayer*. It's praying, but with and through a pen. It's a time to be with God and "discuss" spiritual matters. It's a time to converse with Jesus, give thanks, pray for others, track your spiritual progress, explore your faith, flesh out those Holy Spirit elbows you keep feeling in your ribs, reflect on Scripture, and dive deeper into your relationship with God. It's a place to record your spiritual goals and spiritual questions. It's a place to review those sins that seem to repeat themselves and a place to feel God's mercy for the forgiveness of those sins. It's a way to discern your gifts and talents and how to use them to build God's kingdom here on earth. It's a place to document observations, personal reflections, and notes on books you are studying. You can save your inspired realizations (I call them "Holy Whispers"—more on those later). You can log your spiritual growth and the healings you have experienced. And you can simply have a conversation with the Father. Or Jesus. Or the Holy Spirit—whatever you feel like doing when you open your notebook. The possibilities are endless! It is your alone time with Jesus and your opportunity to be still and learn from him. No annoying brothers (or cute boys) allowed.

*I have no idea what to write.* Lucky you! You are holding in your pretty hands a book that will give you plenty of easy writing ideas, prompts, and formats to try. You won't be interested in all of them, and some of them will not fit your style. But there will be a few ideas that will speak to you, and you'll say to yourself, "Hey, maybe I can try that." God doesn't care what you write. He already knows what's on your mind anyway! Just pick something and run with it. If you don't like the way you are writing today, you get to try something else tomorrow. And just to show you how easy this process is, I've included Prayer Journaling Practice questions at the end of each chapter, so you can ease into it without any hitches.

*Whew!* Have I shot down all your objections? I hope so!

I think you are ready for this adventure, girlfriend, so scrap those worries and let's get started. Be not afraid! God is seeking you, but his invitation requires your response. Say yes!

One quick note before we move on: When you begin prayer journaling, you will soon realize you are not in your "prayer chair" by yourself. You will have an army of cheerleaders alongside you! You'll have the help of Father, Son, Holy Spirit, Mother Mary, and all the saints and angels. Plus, St. Thérèse of Lisieux, St. John XXIII, St. Faustina, St. Ignatius, St. Teresa of Calcutta and many other saints reportedly kept journals, so they all have your back for sure. Let's also ask for the special intercession of the patron saint of journalists and writers as we jump into this process: St. Francis de Sales, pray for us!

### COOL CATHOLIC QUOTE:

*"God takes pleasure to see you take your little steps;*
*and like a good father who holds his child by the hand,*
*he will accommodate his steps to yours and will be content*
*to go no faster than you. Why do you worry?"*
St. Francis de Sales[5]

### PRAYER JOURNALING PRACTICE

Do you have resistance to the idea of prayer journaling?
Any hurdles? Objections? Hesitations?
Jot them down in your new prayer journal and
write a little prayer to God to help you overcome them.

# Two

## BE QUIET!

*Be still, and know that I am God.*

*Psalm 46:10*

When I was growing up in a rowdy household with three older brothers and a younger sister, my mom had a strict rule that we were never allowed to say "shut up" to each other (or anyone else, for that matter). This meant that I had to come up with a creative alternative when my brothers teased me nonstop about my freckles or my sister pestered me with questions while I was trying to do something really important (like put on makeup to cover those freckles). I became an expert at squinting my eyes in an evil way and hissing through my teeth. "Be *quiiiettttt!*" I would warn with all my teenage fury, and the offending party would slink away.

I sincerely doubt that's what my mom had in mind.

In this chapter I'm going to tell you that *you* need to *be quiet* too, only now I am saying it in a much nicer manner, without any squinting or hissing, and I hope and pray you do not slink away.

## GET AWAY FROM YOUR CROWDS

You already know this: It's important to get quiet and be quiet—to set aside a silent, focused time to pray. We must get away from the hustle and bustle of our everyday lives and go on a mini-retreat with God on a regular basis. Even Jesus had to get away! The Bible cites a number of times during Jesus's ministry on earth when he left the crowds and went off to pray and talk with his Father. If Jesus Christ himself needed alone time with his Father, we mere mortals certainly need it even more! It's crucial to our faith lives. But it's not easy.

Jesus knows it isn't easy. Often when he was by himself praying, his disciples would come looking for him or the crowds seeking more miracle healings would discover where he was and press in on him. You may not have crowds of people pressing in on you and begging for miracles, but you likely have a crowd of family members around who each want a piece of you. Plus, you have to get your day started. And let me guess—your mind is already racing before your eyes are even open in the morning. Thoughts of meetings, projects, and deadlines at work can crowd in too. And then there's the housework and the groceries and all the appointments. Yeah, that can all add up and make it feel like the walls are closing in. Who has time to be still?

The answer, of course, is *all of us*. We all have time to be still and converse with God. Our new friend St. Francis de Sales says it best: "Every one of us needs half an hour of prayer each day, except when we are busy—then we need an hour."[6] Nailed it once again, St. Francis!

The problem? Being still is not a practice that is honored in our culture. We are taught to worship the gods of technology and multitasking. We are told that being constantly busy equals being productive and successful. We are bombarded with noise from every angle, practically all day long. But if we continually find ourselves in the middle of all that chaos, we can easily be drawn away from God and our faith. I know this; I used to be hooked on all that stimulation too. And it was definitely not conducive to a strong spiritual life.

When life is busy and messy and chaotic and loud (which can be most of the time), we need all the more to be still. That's the ideal time for us to stop and pray. To get away. To be quiet. To be alone with God so we can learn to recognize when it's his voice telling us what choices to make and which path to take. You can't get to know someone's voice or have a good conversation with them when there's too much noise in the background.

Are you a mom? Did you ever take your child to a birthday party at a pizza joint filled with maniacal arcade games and featuring a giant mouse who performs cheesy skits on a stage? Did you ever try to have a civil, meaningful conversation with any adult at this same party? Of course you didn't. It just does *not* work. You are too occupied chasing children, trying not to have a seizure from all the blinking lights, and attempting to wipe up the spill your child just made with the supposedly spill-proof cup. The same is true of your everyday circumstances. There is often just too much going on throughout your day to have a deep and lengthy time-out with Jesus. That doesn't mean you can't have conversations with him on the fly throughout your day. He wants that too! But if you really want to talk to (and really want to listen to) someone—and become friends with them—you must focus your attention on that person and minimize your distractions as much as possible. We need to get away from the chaos and meet God in silence. St. Teresa of Calcutta tells it like it is:

> We cannot find God in noise or agitation. Nature: trees, flowers and grass grow in silence. The stars, the moon and the sun move in silence. What is essential is not what we say but what God tells others through us. In silence He listens to us; in silence He speaks to our souls. In silence we are granted the privilege of listening to His voice. Silence of our eyes. Silence of our ears. Silence of our minds. . . . In the silence of our heart God will speak.[7]

Are you familiar with the term *white space?* It's a concept I learned during my marketing and advertising career. It means advertisers shouldn't cram a print ad with all kinds of pictures and information. They need to leave room for the readers' eyes to move freely so they can absorb the information more readily. Our brains don't respond well when the content is too dense and too complex. Ad designers need to intentionally create "white space" in the ad where no content exists in order for the advertising to be most effective.

We human beings need white space too: *spiritual* white space. Intentional breaks and gaps and pauses in our day, every day, to turn to heaven and talk to our God in order to grow in our spiritual life. Our lives need white space. Our brains need white space. Our souls need white space. I know you get this. It makes perfect sense. I'm just restating (nagging?) so you will commit to creating it in your life.

## MORNING GLORY

Now that we are all on the same page about the necessity of making time to be quiet with God, I'm going to throw a curve ball at you: *Do it in the morning.*

That's right. The crazy author of this book is actually suggesting you make time to journal with your Father in the morning, perhaps right in the thick of the most unpredictable part of your day. What's up with that and how in the world is this going to work?

I recently read that what a person does before 9:00 a.m. every morning sets the tone for her entire day. Not only that, it sets the tone for her week, her month, her year, and her *life.* According to Laura Vanderkam in her best-selling book, *What the Most Successful People Do Before Breakfast*, "Mornings seem to be made for getting things done."[8] In particular, her research tells us that tasks requiring self-discipline (*hello, prayer journaling!*) are simply easier to do when the day is young. "In the morning . . . the supply of willpower is fresh. . . . In these early hours, we have enough willpower and energy to tackle things that require internal motivation, things the outside world does not immediately demand or reward . . ."[9] She goes on to say that "the best morning rituals are activities that, when practiced regularly, result in long-term benefits."[10] Doesn't that sound like a good description of prayer journaling?

If you need a little more convincing, turn to Psalm 5:3: "O Lord, in the morning thou dost hear my voice; in the morning I prepare a sacrifice for thee, and watch." Many centuries ago, the Psalmist blocked out time in the morning to praise and worship and talk with God. We should take his advice! The rest of your day will be enhanced when you begin it with the Lord. Adriene, a young mother of four, agrees:

> My personal favorite time to prayer journal is in the quiet of the morning before the busyness of the day begins. If you start your day with an intimate conversation with Jesus through prayer journaling, it sets your mind on *him*. All throughout my day I find myself drifting back to thoughts I had written down earlier. I have realized when I don't make the time to prayer journal in the morning, the rest of my day suffers. My best days begin in prayer and end in prayer.

Jackie, a business owner with three adult children and two grandkids, concurs:

> I try to do my devotions, journaling, etc., the same time every day, preferably in the morning. I feel as though God should have the first part of my day, and often my day goes a lot better because of it.

## AVOID THE QUICKSAND

Bottom line: It's a matter of reworking and re-prioritizing our schedules. How do we do that? In her book, *Walking with Purpose*,

Lisa Brenninkmeyer acknowledges the power of the world to draw us busy women away from the important activities that have eternal value. She offers this advice:

> As you look at your daily schedule, ask yourself why you are doing what you do. The key to determining where you should spend your time lies in your motivation and your priorities. Do these things have eternal value? If you were to cut out certain activities, would you be able to find more time to do the things that really matter?[11]

This is food for thought, girlfriend. Your number one priority is your relationship with God, right? Spending quiet time with him has eternal value. It really matters.

Think about your mornings right now. What can you do to "find" more time? Can you move some activities to the night before? Or set your alarm earlier? What are your "time-wasters"? TV? Social media? Hitting the snooze button too often? Lack of planning the night before? Checking your phone way too much? I'm guilty of all of the above. These habits have an insidious way of growing out of control and shoving aside the better stuff like a good breakfast, calm send-offs for our spouse and children, exercise, and prayer journaling. They are quicksand.

When I was a kid, my brothers and I were fascinated by the plethora of TV characters who found themselves mired in a mysterious bog of quicksand. We were taking no chances: When my parents were out, we practiced avoiding "quicksand" by jumping from couch to chair to desk from one end of the house to the other. The only way we could touch the floor was if we threw down a pillow and used it as a stepping-stone to the next piece of furniture. We wanted to be fully prepared if and when we met up with real quicksand! Little did I know that the more threatening quicksand in my life would not be the literal kind. The real quicksand is the distractions and endless to-dos that pull me away and bog me down and keep me from the eternally important things.

What is your quicksand? How can you avoid it? Throw down your pillows and step over that quicksand, friend! Don't let it drag you under. Do whatever you need to do to take back your mornings and offer them to God.

## GIVE IT UP

This won't be a walk in the park. Developing a prayer life in the morning often means we have to sacrifice something else. When I was working fifty-plus hours a week at a high-stress job in the banking industry, I typically found myself sitting around a boardroom table with mostly men whose wives worked at home. When we needed to schedule additional meetings, these men often requested breakfast get-togethers, say around 7:30 a.m. That time of day posed no problem for them, but I always balked at it. Nope, no early morning meetings for me. They probably thought I was being un-ambitious and uncoopera-tive and a few other things. But what I was really doing was protecting my morning time. They were all great, hardworking colleagues, but they had no clue how much work I put in prior to coming to work! By the time I got to my office, I felt like I was clocking in to my second shift of the day. I gave up looking like a team player to my colleagues so I could exercise a bit, pick up the house, get my children off to school with no calls to 911, and spend precious prayer journaling time with my God—my "first shift" priorities.

I also had to take a good, hard look at my TV-watching habits. A few years back I read some astounding statistics on the number of hours the average American spends watching television, and I was convicted. At the time, I was trying to handle all the responsibilities of being a good wife, mother, and employee plus trying to launch a new magazine on the side, and can I just say it was not working out. There were not enough hours in the day! It was Lent—a good time to try a little sacrifice—so I radically reduced the amount of time the TV was on in the house, even if I only had it on for background noise. Before you get the idea that I am a holier-than-thou, goody-two-shoes who can easily change her long-standing bad habits for the better, I should probably mention that this was also about the time that we got a new TV and the number of remotes on our coffee table hit critical mass. I could no longer figure out how to operate our television. So, yeah, some of the decrease in viewing time was involuntary. But once I did cut down on it, somehow, magically, my schedule opened up! I didn't miss the shows, which mostly turn our brains to mush anyway, and I found the time to do what I needed to do. I highly recommend this option, whether or not you actually know how to turn on your TV.

My new prayer journaling compadre, I am confident that you can identify and corral your distractions and to-do lists and find the extra time so you can try prayer journaling in the morning.

You really will enjoy starting your day with God if you can make a few adjustments. As Debbie Guardino says:

> If all you did was talk to your husband for an hour a week, you wouldn't have much of a relationship with him. Relationships need investment. If you want to grow in this relationship, you have to invest in the time. Even five minutes to start your day. It's never going to be easy—the enemy tries to get in the way. But being able to start your day this way is a huge benefit.

Ask God for help to find time and avoid quicksand—he will always answer that prayer. And be assured that your efforts to arrange special time with him will not go unnoticed or unrewarded. There are countless times in my prayer journal that I've remarked how God has cleared a path for me to get everything accomplished even after spending prized morning time with him: Work will flow unusually smoothly, a meeting or event will get cancelled, or a "to-do" list item will no longer be needed. Something always happens to free up my schedule. I call it his "way-making," and it never fails to make me smile.

Setting aside time for prayer journaling in the morning will be rewarding and even refreshing. The day starts better, goes better, and ends better when we dedicate some morning time to praying with a pen.

Be refreshed. Be still. *Be quiet.*

### COOL CATHOLIC QUOTE:

*"Each day we need a time that is set aside exclusively for prayer. Christian life is simply not sustainable without it."*
*Matthew Kelly,* Rediscover Jesus [12]

### PRAYER JOURNALING PRACTICE

Take a look at your schedule. How can you find two or three ways to create more time in the mornings?

What is your quicksand? How can you step over or around it? Use your prayer journal to converse with God about your obstacles to morning prayer journaling time.

# Three

## A SIMPLE START—THE FOUR P'S OF PRAYING WITH A PEN

*Rejoice in hope, endure in affliction, persevere in prayer.*
*Romans 12:12*

Here are some of the best things about your new habit of praying with a pen:

- It costs very little.
- It requires no class attendance.
- You don't need to make a trip to a hobby store, subscribe to a magazine, or even pay any dues.

We are not going to make this complicated, sister. If you're like me, if something gets too complicated, you have trouble sticking with it. Prayer journaling is supposed to be stress-free—let's keep it that way!

All you really need to begin this new habit are the Four Ps: Pen, Paper, Place, and Persistence. The first three are fairly painless and straightforward. The last one, well, not so much.

## THE PEN

Let's start with the basics, shall we? First, your writing instrument: Pick what makes you happy, friend. If you are "old school" and enjoy the sound of pencil lead scratching on paper, grab a sharp pencil and have at it. If you want to buy an elegant, special pen to use for this purpose, feel free. If you have a favorite pen that you have to hide from everyone else in the household (along with the good pair of scissors and a stash of emergency chocolate), that sounds like the pen you should use to write to God.

Did you notice that I did not mention a PC, laptop, smartphone, or tablet as a way to capture your prayer journaling thoughts? There's a good reason for that: I don't want you to use those options! This is not just me being bossy (although I do have that tendency). I love my tech tools too. But I think prayer journaling is best done by hand, the old-fashioned way. Why? It's that research thing again.

Writing in longhand has a different effect on your brain than punching keys on a keyboard does. It activates more regions of the brain, stimulates more creativity, and helps us better retain information. A *Wall Street Journal* story noted this phenomenon. In it, Virginia Berninger, a professor of educational psychology at the University of Washington, states that handwriting differs from typing because it requires "executing sequential strokes to form a letter, whereas keyboarding involves selecting a whole letter by touching a key."[13] She says pictures of the brain illustrate that those sequential finger movements activate massive regions involved in thinking, language, and working memory—the system we all use for temporarily storing and managing information. And one recent study of hers demonstrated that in grades two, four, and six, children wrote more words faster and expressed more ideas when writing essays by hand than when writing with a keyboard.[14] In addition, two university research scientists, Pam Mueller and Daniel Oppenheimer, conducted experiments and came to conclusions that also seem to support longhand over typing when it comes to retaining information. In three studies, they found that college students who took notes on laptops performed worse on conceptual questions than students who took notes by hand.[15]

In other words, my friend, if you really want to engage your brain when journaling, handwriting works best. A goal with prayer journaling is to be as open and receptive as possible. We want our thoughts and ideas to flow freely, and we want the Holy Spirit to have total access. It appears that the act of traditional handwriting can help with this. Engaging multiple areas of your brain by using a pen can let you connect more openly with God and more easily recall the interaction.

It's not impossible to do that on a computer or smartphone, of course. Many people journal and blog and even write whole books about God and to God that way. If you feel you must do it electronically, do it electronically. But I encourage you to give handwriting a try. In addition to the brain-to-hand research, we know handwriting is more personal. (Don't we love getting a handwritten note from our spouse or our child?) And prayer journaling is, beyond all the research findings, a personal endeavor.

## THE PAPER

Now, on to the paper. Again, it's simple: Use whatever you prefer. Head on out to the dollar store and buy a composition notebook like the kind you had in grade school. Or buy a journal with a hard cover and pretty paper inside. Or use a three-ring binder with tabbed dividers to organize specific sections of your journal. You can go online and search for printable prayer journal pages to use with your binder. You can also get super creative and decorate your prayer journal, "scrapbook-style"—just be careful not to add stress to the process or get distracted from the purpose by getting too fancy with it. The only other caution I would give is to not go too big or bulky—there will be times you may need to take this notebook on a road trip or vacation, so it should be fairly portable and fit comfortably in your lap. And, if you're like me, you will not be able to bear throwing out any of your old prayer journals—they will contain the powerful story of your spiritual growth. Storage will be easier with smaller notebooks.

## THE PLACE

How's it sounding so far? Manageable? Not too stressful? Good.

Let's talk about the place for your prayer journaling: Make it as private as possible, and mark it as yours and yours alone. OK, you can let your cat or dog join you. But other than that, you need to find a place that you can commandeer for yourself. You will want to keep your journals and your resources handy in this place, so it needs to be somewhat remote. Move a comfy chair to a corner of your bedroom. Use a spare bedroom. Fix up an area in your basement or attic or even your closet—anywhere you won't be disturbed for your ten, fifteen, or thirty minutes of daily prayer journaling.

The privacy and seclusion of your prayer journaling spot is important. St. Teresa of Avila was well aware of this need:

> However quietly we speak, God is so near that we will be heard. We need no wings to go in search of God, but have only to find a place where we can be alone and look upon the presence within us.[16]

Find your place! You want to relax and concentrate—you can't do that with the din of family life swirling all around you. Jesus instructed us on this topic, right before he gave us the words to the Lord's Prayer in Matthew 6:6: "But when you pray, go into your room and shut the door and pray to your Father who is in secret; and your Father who sees in secret will reward you." While Jesus may not have meant a literal room, I do think it means that designating a private, quiet spot for prayer journaling would be beneficial, don't you?

I have created a special corner off my bedroom for prayer journaling. I share the area with a dust-covered sewing machine. (If I try hard enough, I can picture it as something a lot more fun—like an ice-cream machine.) After a few years of using a rocker, I purchased a small chaise lounge on clearance and placed it next to a bookcase and a little table that holds a candle, a wedding photo, a plant, a rosary, and a box of tissues.

I have found each of these accessories to be both inspiring and useful at different times and in different ways. In addition to my treasured book collection, the bookcase also displays vacation photos, encouraging verses, a framed drawing of the Virgin Mary that I got for free at a garage sale, and a prayer jar that holds little slips of paper with my special prayer intentions. Across from me, at eye level, hangs a small crucifix.

On the chaise lounge is a basket that holds my notebook, extra pens, devotionals, a Catholic Bible, various other journaling tools we will discuss in a later chapter, and my Kindle. I don't prefer reading books on a device but, sister, if I didn't own a Kindle, my house would have been completely overrun with books by now (I have a problem). Draped across the back of my chair is an angel-themed blanket that I received from friends when my dad passed away. And off to the side is a soft yellow prayer shawl that a church member crocheted for us when my husband's father passed away.

When you have selected your spot, work your own brand of homemaking magic on it. Surround yourself with things you love. This is *your* retreat, girlfriend! Make it look and feel that way. You will be more motivated to spend time there if you love how it feels when you are seated there. Add to the sacred feeling of your space too. Maybe you have a beautiful statue of Mary that comforts you—put her nearby. Add a candle, a crucifix, some prayer cards, even a holy water font if you wish. And finally, make sure everyone knows this is *your* private haven. No exceptions! My son can testify to this. He got squawked at once when I found him sitting in my prayer journaling area, innocently looking for a book in my bookcase. Sorry, kiddo—this is my place, my sanctuary! Your prayer place is your sanctuary too. This is where you go to meet God—it should be valued and protected like Fort Knox—minus the weaponry, of course.

## PERSISTENCE

This is the tough one, my prayer journaling friend. We humans often find it difficult to finish what we start. And who can blame us? Our throw-away, hurry-up society discourages persistence. We like to move on quickly and find the next big trend or item or idea—or person. Lengthy marriages are rare and are celebrated as anomalies. And our attention spans? Practically nonexistent. But here's the thing: Persistence is vital to a prayer journaling habit. Persistence means committing fully. Jumping in with both feet. Going all in. It's the only way to see any results. The growth you are seeking will not come overnight or from a sporadic commitment. The relationship you want to develop with Jesus will take dedication. As prayer journaler Adriene notes, "The thing is, unless one is *intentional* about spending time with him, it's hard to hear what he is trying to say." There's no way to sugarcoat it, girlfriend: A rewarding prayer journaling experience requires great persistence.

Have you ever suffered an injury or ailment that left you in chronic pain? When I hit forty-five years old, my body decided the joyride was over and it was payback time for all those years of neglect. In particular, the discs in my lower back decided to make their presence known. It took two years of doctor visits, MRIs, chiropractic care, shots, and physical therapy to get my back, well, back. But in order to keep it that way, I have to do daily stretching exercises. My back hurts if I don't stretch it regularly. In much the same way, my life begins to develop spiritual aches and pains when I am not in close communication with God every day. I don't want to return to a life of chronic pain, so I do my daily exercises. I don't want to go back to a spiritually dry life, so I stay on top of my prayer journaling and other activities that build my faith life. A healthy body requires intention and persistence. A healthy spiritual life requires intention and persistence too.

## BEGIN AGAIN. AND AGAIN. AND AGAIN.

You won't be perfect at prayer journaling every day, especially when you're just getting started, and that's OK. There will be times when it doesn't work. You will deal with sickness, emergencies, travel, unavoidable schedule changes and, in my case, just plain forgetfulness. And let's not discount the power of our old friend "resistance"—that human tendency to avoid doing something that we know is good for us. In his book *Resisting Happiness*, Matthew Kelly tells us, "In every moment of every day, resistance is there, waiting to pounce. . . . [Resistance] causes us to settle for so much less than God has imagined for us."[17]

When this happens, don't beat up on yourself. God allows do-overs. He is the master at encouraging what I call "begin-agains." Just think about the beautiful sacrament of Reconciliation that he created for us. He is a merciful God who understands our fallen nature and is always ready and able to forgive and provide us with the strength to begin again!

Know that you are not alone in your struggle to be quiet and carve out time to be with God. "Finding time is probably one of the hardest parts of prayer journaling," said Diane, a fifty-something elementary school teacher, wife, mom, grandma, Catholic, and prayer journaler. "It is even harder when you have little ones and more distractions. It helps to remember that Jesus is there any time we come to him. I know that whenever I make the time to prayer journal, he will be there waiting for me."

He wants you back in your prayer chair so you can speak to him and he can speak to you. Tomorrow is a new day. Begin again.

Want to make it easier to be persistent? Start small. Five minutes a day is a realistic goal to launch your prayer journaling habit, and then work your way up to fifteen minutes or so if and when you can. Give yourself a break; it will take some starts and stops before you get the hang of this. The experts tell us it takes twenty-one days to fully form a new habit. Set an alarm, schedule it, put reminders in your phone or on your watch, put a sticky note on your bathroom mirror—use whatever means necessary to help you develop this new habit.

We have to be a little like Dory, the loveable, always-confused fish from the Disney movie, *Finding Nemo*.[18] One of her favorite sayings in the face of difficulty, which has now become one of my favorite sayings in the face of difficulty, is "Just keep swimming, swimming, swimming." Be Dory: Just keep writing, no matter how you feel, no matter how full your day will be, no matter if it's been a week since you last journaled. Muscle through. *Just keep swimming!* As the saying goes, persistence pays off. You will be rewarded for hanging in there.

Prayer journaler Jackie is familiar with these rewards. "Prayer journaling has helped me focus more on him and less on me. Oftentimes it turns my 'pity party' into a 'praise party.'"

"Prayer journaling helps keep me centered and focused on him," fellow journaler Adriene says. "It slows down my thoughts and helps me connect with Jesus in a way I never knew possible. I can honestly say prayer journaling has been the best way for me to develop my personal relationship with Jesus."

The same goes for me; I have experienced each of these benefits as well. You will too if you stay with it!

Still concerned about your ability to persist? Here's the silver bullet you've been waiting for: You can use your prayer journaling time to ask for the courage and perseverance to stick to your prayer journaling time! Galatians 6:9 tells us, "And let us not grow weary in well-doing, for in due season we shall reap, if we do not lose heart." If you are growing tired, don't give up! Ask for the perseverance! Open your notebook and begin by writing something like, "This is hard, God. I'm all fuzzy-brained and time-crunched right now. I don't know if I can commit to this. Holy Spirit, please help me be persistent. Please give me the fortitude to use this time today and every day to talk to you and listen to you and get to know you better." God will supply what you need to persevere, and before you know it, the ink will be flowing and you will reap a harvest, just as Galatians 6:9 promises.

## COOL CATHOLIC QUOTE:

*"Perseverance in prayer keeps our faith alive and strong.*
*For in that prayer, we experience the compassion of God who,*
*like a Father filled with love and mercy,*
*is ever ready to come to the aid of his children."*
*Pope Francis[19]*

## PRAYER JOURNALING PRACTICE

Take some time to plan your ideal prayer corner and
gather your supplies. What will your space look like?
What favorite items will you include?

Now, set your timer for five minutes and write from your
chosen spot. Don't think about it—just say hello to
God and keep on writing. How did it go?

# *Four*

## DO IT LIKE THIS (IF YOU WANT TO)

*This is the day which the Lord has made; let us rejoice and be glad in it.*
*Psalm 118:24*

Warning: This is the only time in this entire book that I will be hardcore insistent and offer a definitive rule when it comes to how you conduct your prayer journaling. Ready? The rule is: *There are no rules.* Prayer journaling is a *personal* way for you to talk to God, which means it gets to be done in a way that suits you well. There is no editor. No agenda. No time requirement. No style restrictions. You get to write the way you write best— sentences or bullet points or even drawings. You can develop your own methods, your favorite resources, your particular approach to your journaling time with Jesus.

Don't worry about getting stuck in a rut—you can change up your prayer journaling practice whenever you want. In fact, you can expect your routine to change as time goes on. You'll try new things, integrate different prayers, and test some devotions you just discovered. You may begin reviewing a book and decide halfway through it that it's not clicking with you, so you switch to something else. You'll develop a rhythm that may work well for one season of your life but must be adapted to the next season. All of this is perfectly fine, and it's actually a good way to keep things interesting.

As I mentioned in the introduction of this book, many years ago I started out writing in the mornings, but not for the sole purpose of prayer journaling. Writing three Morning Pages got me in the groove of writing every day. But God had other plans, better plans, for my morning writing routine. I mean, you're holding a book that I have written about Catholic prayer journaling, for crying out loud! If that's not an unimaginable ending to an unassuming beginning, I don't know what is. I went from purposeless, stream-of-consciousness writing on a wide variety of subjects in order to get my creative juices flowing and become a better writer to nothing but thirty minutes of prayer journaling every morning. I never would have dreamed that those first baby steps I took into the realm of journaling would end up in daily, personal, private conversation with God the way it has. I couldn't be more delighted with the evolution.

The habit of prayer journaling will be the source of much delight in your life too. Your growth and development as a disciple of prayer journaling may not end in a book publishing deal, but don't be surprised by the gifts God has in store just for you within the pages of a simple notebook.

And now (drumroll, please)—it's the moment you've been waiting for! I'm going to share with you how I usually spend my prayer journaling time. Feel free to copy, borrow, or steal any of these ideas or use them as inspiration for your own routine.

Or feel free to ignore all of it and do your own thing. It's your call.

## MY PRAYER JOURNALING ROUTINE

My husband's alarm clock blares country music at 6:05 a.m. every morning. I mutter a few unintelligible things, and then he hits the snooze button. But by 6:15 he is out of bed and all that movement and noise compels me to get up too. I gingerly lift my little dog Sammy out of bed. (Yes, he sleeps with us. On his back. With all four paws in the air.) And then I stand at the window next to my bed. I draw open the curtains and shades and soak up the light and make a Sign of the Cross, silently thanking God for letting me witness another morning. I then stumble to the front door, let the dog out, hit the bathroom, pull on some semi-reasonable clothing, shuffle into the kitchen to get a tall glass of flavored ice water, take my vitamins and medicine for the day, and let the dog back in. Hubby and I make the bed and then sit at the edge to have a quick devotional time together before he goes off to slay his dragons. By now it's 6:45 or so, and it's time to prayer journal. There's no TV, no radio, no newspaper, no Internet, no smartphone before I sit down for prayer journaling—I don't want any outside influences to color my time with Jesus. And even though I'm tempted to quickly throw in a load of laundry or do some other task, I resist.

Do you notice anything missing from my current morning description? Like, say, the pandemonium of taking care of children? Well, that's because I'm now fifty-something, and my kids are out of the nest. But I have been journaling in the mornings for many years, right on through the preschool, elementary, high school, and college phases. I was usually up at 6:00 a.m. or earlier back then, without the luxury of extra sleep and with the need to get the bambinos off to school and get myself ready for work. It can be done, believe me, even if you have to journal in bed as soon as you wake up. In fact, you may appreciate the restful, battery-charging, encouraging time with Jesus even more during the "kids-at-home" days.

## GETTING INTO A GROOVE

Am I now ready to settle down and start writing? Not quite yet. If you're like me, you can't just plop down on a comfy chair and start in. I may be headed to a quiet, calm location, but my brain is far from quiet. It's hopping and bopping and objecting to the request to chill. Do you have this issue too? I understand completely. I often compare my brain to a pinball machine on crack (and I don't even drink coffee! Oh, what my brain would be like on caffeine . . .). It's *so hard* to get it to stop pinging and dinging. It wants to jump out of the chute and get the game started for the day. That's definitely not helpful when I need to settle down for prayer journaling. Here's what I have learned: When one has a pinball brain, one has no choice but to trick that pinball brain into submission.

If you ever had a three-year-old who did not want to go to bed, you will identify with this technique. The experts tell you it's all about how you prepare the child for bedtime: Have a set bedtime. Give the bath, put on the jammies, read the story, get the drink of water, sing a song, say the prayers. Every. Single. Night. It's called *routine*. For some reason our brains like knowing what to expect. So, when I enter my little prayer corner, I try to do the same physical actions every day. It's my pre-journaling warm-up. I walk slowly to the window and adjust the shades. I turn on the table lamp. I set down my drink, take a seat on the chair, and turn to the side to catch my little Sammy mid-jump as he joins me. I pet him for a bit, and then I grab that prayer shawl and throw it across my legs. I light a candle. And then I take a slow, deep breath, close my eyes, and make the Sign of the Cross.

This kind of mind-body routine works, friend. My husband can vouch for it. He was a high school varsity boys' basketball coach for many years. They played a tough schedule that required the teenage boys to be not only physically prepared but also mentally prepared (no small task, given all that testosterone). Without fail, the coaches made sure the team's pregame ritual was the same prior to every game. The drills were the same, the background music blaring in the gym was the same, the prayers in the huddle were the same, even the type of gum my husband handed out to his players before the National Anthem was the same—Juicy Fruit, *always* Juicy Fruit. The boys knew what to expect and how things were going to go, so they could quiet their brains enough to prepare for the challenge ahead of them.

You may not need Juicy Fruit gum or a peppy fight song, but you may need to establish a brief physical routine to be prepared for your prayer journaling time. Every little bit helps!

## DUMPING THOSE DISTRACTIONS

So, finally, my body is quiet. I am seated on my chair, the notebook is in my lap and my pen is poised. But I have to take care of one more housekeeping detail to put the brakes on my pinball brain even more—something I learned early on from Morning Pages. I have to first "dump" whatever is still buzzing in the forefront of my mind—a leftover dream segment, an urgent something that I need to note or it will bug me, or, most often, um, the song that's playing in my head. Yes, I am telling you that many of my prayer journaling entries begin with un-profound statements such as: *Flea medicine; Wow, that was one bizarre dream;* or *I like that old-time rock and roll, that kind of music just soothes the soul.* I find it quite hilarious to read these notes whenever I review my journals (A little comic relief is always a good thing). But I know these initial notations are a necessary part of the process for me. They sweep the final mental clutter out of the way and clear the path to talk with Jesus. This is what you do with mental distractions, especially at the beginning of your prayer time. You acknowledge them, you dump them, and then you move on to better things.

St. Teresa of Avila—who was a doctor of the Church and quite a practical woman, I might add—was familiar with dealing with distractions during prayer. In her writings she counsels us:

> [I]t is impossible to speak to God and to the world at the same time; yet this is just what we are trying to do when we are saying our prayers and at the same time listening to the conversation of others or letting our thoughts wander on any matter that occurs to us, without making an effort to control them.[20]

But have no fear—she wrote in *The Interior Castle*: "We should not be distressed by reason of our thoughts, nor allow ourselves to be worried by them. . . . [Thoughts are] inevitable. Do not let them disturb or grieve you."[21]

In other words—don't worry about it! Distractions are not sinful (although the devil himself may be trying to get you off track. I'm sure he intensely resents the practice of prayer journaling). We just have to do something about them. And if you're prone to passing "Squirrel!" thoughts like I am, dealing with them is not optional. You acknowledge the distracting squirrels, you catch them, and then you release them quickly, hopefully to run off into the woods and stop bothering you. Distractions are a fact of prayer life. But take heart. St. Teresa continues:

> Do not imagine that the important thing is never to be thinking of anything else and that if your mind becomes slightly distracted all is lost . . . [T]hink of distractions as mere clouds passing in the sky, momentarily taking your gaze from the Sun of Righteousness . . . [22]

Admittedly, my analogies of squirrel-bagging are much less eloquent than St. Teresa's advice on handling distractions, but you get my drift. Figure out how to best give your thoughts and your emotions (and don't forget those pesky, fluctuating hormones!) a little pre-journaling pep talk—letting them know you are about to do something very important and you would appreciate their full cooperation, thank you very much. Do what *you* need to do to quiet your mind and deal with your distractions—if you don't, you will only be frustrated with your prayer journaling experience.

## GETTING DOWN TO BUSINESS

After I have quickly disposed of my distractions, I am finally ready to write. If you're thinking at this point that I begin a lengthy, spiritually powerful, in-depth, articulate conversation with God, well, you would be wrong. I usually write something very inelegant like *Good morning, God—how are you?* Then I write something like *Thanks for another beautiful day. Help me to live it the way you want me to.* And then off I go on my typically three-page, free-for-all conversation with the Holy Trinity.

What's on those three pages? I usually take a look ahead and ask God to help me through the challenges of the day: a tough meeting, a house full of kids, a difficult conversation with an aging parent. Even a trip to the grocery store lands on my prayer list, as I despise grocery shopping. I may bring up something that happened to me the previous day and try to see what fresh perspective Jesus has for me. Sometimes I pick just one word that's bouncing around in my head—like *joy*, or *ponder*, or *worry*—and write about it. Other times I ask intercessions for friends and family, say thanks for the good things that happened over the last twenty-four hours, take a minute to give God praise, or simply ask a question that's been on my mind, such as: *How can I better handle this coworker? Why did I give in to the temptation to gossip yesterday? Should I take on this new opportunity? How do you put up with me?* I can usually work through an answer on the following pages, even though that last one is a doozy.

We can talk to Jesus about anything! I express my frustrations—with life, with others, with myself. I confess sins and ask for forgiveness and keep a list of sins I want to discuss the next time I go to confession. And I often duke it out with my unwanted companions—what I call the three D's of discouragement, doubt, and disappointment—right there on those pages. I ask the Holy Spirit for grace and mercy and strength. I ask for insight. And I ask for a sense of humor and joy and a light heart to carry me through the day. None of this is in any certain order—Morning Pages taught me to just put my pen down on the paper and never let up. You can do it in any order you want.

## LISTENING FOR HOLY WHISPERS

By the third page, I am ready to stop talking and start listening a bit more to what God wants to say to me. It *is* supposed to be a conversation, after all; I shouldn't be doing all the talking. When God does the talking in my journal, I call that hearing Holy Whispers. You'll have the same experience when you prayer journal—I can almost guarantee it. You'll be chugging along, maybe reading the Gospel for the day, pondering a problem, or asking a question from your heart when suddenly, *ding!* A Holy Whisper in your ear! These are wonderful, thought-provoking gifts from God that make prayer journaling so worthwhile. (See chapter eight for more on recognizing and capturing your Holy Whispers!)

I find prompts and resources useful in getting the two-way conversation going. I pull out a daily calendar with a Scripture verse and jot that down. I stew on it a bit, wondering what it means for me and my day and how I can apply it to my life. I then grab a devotional—usually something tied to the current liturgical season. I read a passage and then immediately write down a thought or reflection on that passage. I try to listen for the lesson God wants to teach me or any Holy Whispers he wants to share with me. And finally, I pull out my Kindle, open the daily Mass readings, and then reflect on the meditation provided. I note a word that spoke to me or a phrase that jumped out at me, and I ask Jesus how the message might be directed at me—more Holy Whispers! When I'm at a good stopping point, I review the last page or so of my journal to see if there's an overarching message in there that I'm supposed to internalize and carry with me over the course of the day. (That's another advantage of journaling while you pray—with a flip of a page you can easily reflect on what you've just prayed about or read.)

*What do I need to know from you right now, Jesus?* is a helpful question for me to pose at this stage. And then it's time to sit quietly once again. I need to give Jesus a chance to answer! When I've done this in the past, very helpful "replies" have often come to me. Once, when contemplating if I was headed in the right direction, the Holy Whisper of understanding I received was this: *Ease. When you are operating with ease, you are doing my will. Pay attention to bumps, detours, restlessness, frustrations. Ease accompanies the alignment of wills.* This is the kind of thing that keeps me coming back every morning. And it will keep you coming back too.

If I sense an answer based on everything I've just read and written and "heard," I try to condense it to one or two words and write it down in my phone or on a sticky note—anywhere I will be able to see it easily throughout the day. For example, I selected the word *ease* on the day I journaled the above Holy Whisper. Many times I jot down the focus word or words on the palm of my hand—I know I won't be going anywhere without that! This is how I try to prevent the drip-drip-drip of "spiritual erosion" throughout the day. No one else can really notice my focus word, but I spy it often during the day and it reminds me of my prayer journal conversation with Jesus that morning.

Finally, I recite the Our Father, make the Sign of the Cross, blow out the candle, and put away my notebook until the next morning.

And there you have it. Nothing wild and crazy or out of the realm of possibility for anyone. It's just me sitting in a corner for a short while, writing and thinking and asking and conversing with Jesus. It's nothing fancy, nothing complicated, nothing intimidating. But the results are immeasurable.

This simple routine has changed my life, dear friend. Through prayer journaling, I've learned how to recognize and tear down walls that stood between me and Jesus (walls I had constructed on my own, of course). I learned how to talk to him, and I learned how to listen for his reply. And I learned that his love for me is endless. On the one hand, it's downright mysterious how a few minutes and a pen and some paper could achieve such a supernatural connection. But on the other hand, it makes perfect sense: God loves us and wants to make it easy to build a relationship with him. We just have to make the initial effort.

## NO WORRIES

Here are things I do not worry about when I sit down to prayer journal (and you shouldn't either): I don't worry about God "standing me up." He's already there, waiting for me. I don't worry about writing something that offends him or makes him retreat—that's impossible. He's a big God and can handle whatever I throw at him. I don't worry about writing eloquently or whether my writing will make sense. God doesn't care. He's just happy I'm there, making the effort to be with him, because (I repeat) I am a beloved daughter—and so are you. And I don't worry about how much time it does or doesn't take. My prayer journaling usually spans about thirty minutes, but if it's less or more, it doesn't matter. How much time should yours take? Whatever works for you. No rules, remember?

I also don't worry about being perfect. "My biggest problem starting out in prayer journaling was thinking I had to be perfect," stated Debbie Guardino. "I actually ripped pages I didn't like out of my journal! I encourage people to get over that one real fast," she told me with a laugh. "It's not being graded."

In the next few chapters we'll take a look at some of the handy resources and methods you can use as you begin to develop your own prayer journaling time. Read on, and be amazed at the magnitude of materials and tools and prompts available to you, all because you belong to the one, holy, catholic, and apostolic Church!

## COOL CATHOLIC QUOTE:
*"There are two ways of waking up in the morning.*
*One is to say, 'Good morning, God.'*
*And the other is to say, 'Good God, morning!'"*
*Venerable Archbishop Fulton Sheen*[23]

## PRAYER JOURNALING PRACTICE
In your prayer journal, list the distractions you anticipate, and pray about how you will deal with each of them.

Write this question in your journal: *What do I need to know from you right now, Jesus?* Listen for his answer.

# Five

## OPEN THE CATHOLIC TREASURE CHEST

*Those who love me I also love, and those who seek me find me.*
*Proverbs 8:17*

Are you still with me? Are you sitting there thinking, "I get it so far, Mary Beth, but how in the world will I ever fill up all the blank pages in this journal?" The answer is—by cheating.

Sort of.

Let me explain.

Back in my marketing and advertising days, I would gather my team together and charge them with coming up with a new advertising campaign. We sat around a big table, new legal pads at the ready. We had a few fits and starts on ideas, but mostly we all stared at each other, and all I heard was "crickets." We had a very difficult time coming up with an idea from scratch. And then I read an article that changed my approach. The next time I gathered my team, the table was full of prompts. We had full-color magazines and catalogs to thumb through; we had sketchbooks and colored pencils; we had promotional items. I turned on some fast-paced music. We played brainstorming games with paper airplanes and modeling clay and Legos. We looked at award-winning advertising samples from companies completely different from ours. And by the time we were finished, we had generated a multitude of very solid and exciting ad campaign concepts! We eliminated the cricket problem by using prompts to help us get our creativity in gear. We dubbed the process "borrowing brilliance." And it worked every time.

In my humble opinion, there is no more brilliant organization on this planet than the Catholic Church. She is bursting at the seams with resources for you to use whenever you pray. She has much to offer those of us who like to journal, whether we are just starting out or have been prayer journaling for years. In this chapter I will list a few favorites that I have found helpful, but first let's clarify something. This will likely not shock you, but . . . I am not a theologian. I am not a Catholic apologist. I am not a catechist. I would describe myself more like a toddler Catholic: I am walking around as best I can, picking up shiny objects as I go, learning new things every day, and falling down an awful lot! Therefore, what I present to you in this chapter is not an exhaustive list of Catholic resources, nor is it meant to be offered in any particular order. It's more of a church basement potluck presentation than it is a seven-course meal served in a sequential manner by people wearing starchy black uniforms. If you don't find something you feel should be included, please don't track me down and say, "Hey, Catholic Prayer Journaling Lady, what about such-and-such?" because here's what I will probably tell you: "If you like using such-and-such, my good sister, and it follows the teachings of the Church, go for it!" And then, I will probably add the such-and-such you mentioned to my *own* list of resources to try next; that's how we roll as prayer journaling girlfriends.

Let's start with some low-hanging fruit—a list of things you may already have on hand and can easily work in to your prayer journaling routine.

## THE CATHOLIC BIBLE

*You guys*—I was embarrassingly old before I realized that not all Bibles are the same (Protestant Bibles have seven fewer books in the Old Testament, thanks to the Reformation. Who knew? Obviously not me.). Catholics have gotten a bad rap in the past for seemingly not studying or even using the Bible (despite the cycle of Mass readings that walk us through almost the entire Bible every three years), but guess what? The Catholic Church can take credit for compiling the original books of the Bible and creating what everyone recognized as the authoritative version for fifteen hundred years. This was no minor accomplishment, especially when everything had to be handwritten back then (and there was no correction fluid or backspace button to correct mistakes!). The Bible is part of your heritage as a Catholic. It's the sacred Word of God. As our prayer journaling friend Adriene noted, "The most important resource I use in prayer journaling is his Word. I use other resources to guide me to places in Scripture. I highlight and then rewrite verses in my journal and note connections I have made to those verses." Get a Catholic Bible! Open it! Read it! Journal with it! Let God speak to you through its pages. He will, believe me.

## THE ROSARY

Of course. You probably received a rosary at your First Communion. Do you know where it is? I'm sorry to say, I had to retrieve mine from a banged-up box in the back of a drawer when I returned to the Catholic Church. I also had to relearn the mysteries of the Rosary (and let me tell you, I was more than a little surprised to find out that there was a whole new set called the Luminous Mysteries and that a Fatima prayer had now been added after the Glory Be. *Where have I been? Oh, yeah . . .*). Friend, do yourself a favor and buy a few extra rosaries and keep one next to your prayer journaling spot. They are inexpensive, and they are invaluable spiritual tools. Look up the mysteries and journal about them. Read a book about the Rosary and reflect on it in your journal. Pray a decade and then pause to record the thoughts you had while praying. Try doing a novena (praying the Rosary nine days straight for a particular intention) and then journaling about the experience. Write about a concern you have, pray all or a segment of the Rosary, and then write about how you feel about the concern afterward. The Rosary is a spiritual weapon you should have in your arsenal at all times.

## BOOKS, DEVOTIONALS, DAILY MASS READINGS

Does your parish have a library? Check it out (pun intended). Go online or visit your favorite local Catholic gift store to purchase good Catholic books and daily devotionals that will get you thinking and asking questions. The supply is nearly endless! My preferred resource for daily Mass readings is *The Word Among Us*. You can get it in a printed booklet or in a digital format on your reader or phone. The daily meditation always seems to hit home and gives me plenty to chew on in my prayer journal. Read selections from the writings of particular saints and other Catholic spiritual giants, perhaps before you go to bed at night. Then, the next morning write about something that may still be stirring in your mind.

## THE CATECHISM OF THE CATHOLIC CHURCH

Yes, I know. It's a huge book. But it's *our* book. We should all get familiar with it. I resisted purchasing one until a priest aimed this question at us in a homily: "Do you have a copy of the *Catechism* in your home? If not, why not?" I had no good answer. So now I have one. And then I learned that the United States Conference of Catholic Bishops (USCCB) offers a "local" adaptation. So I bought *The United States Catholic Catechism for Adults* . . . and I was pleasantly surprised! It was actually an extremely valuable tool for me when I came back to the Church, and it still is. It covers almost everything I want to know, or have questions about, in a very user-friendly fashion. And, for prayer journaling purposes, there are discussion questions, meditations, and prayers posted at the end of each chapter. Both of these resources are also available at no charge online at www.usccb.org. Dig in!

## APPS

Technology has made it easier to be an "integrated" Catholic in many ways, especially when it comes to apps available for your smartphone or other devices. I currently have apps for the Rosary, the Examen, the Divine Mercy Chaplet, novenas, confession and more. With a little bit of search time in your app store, you can find daily inspiration from trusted Catholic sources to help with your prayer journaling. I know I said that using technology isn't the best idea when you prayer journal, but helpful apps are an efficient exception.

## SONG LYRICS

Many of my girlfriends listen to Christian music every single day. They know the meaningful words of hymns and other inspirational songs have the power to evoke feelings of love and gratitude and joy, and remind us that Jesus hears us when we talk to him (and journal to him). How does music affect you? Try choosing a favorite Christian song and dissecting it in your prayer journal, or simply using it as background music as you write.

## RADIO AND TV PROGRAMS

When I came back to the Church, the local Catholic radio station was my classroom. I couldn't get enough. A radio show such as *Catholic Answers* on EWTN radio provided me with much food for thought. Ave Maria Radio and The Catholic Channel on SiriusXM are two other great options. And let's not forget EWTN and CatholicTV—both phenomenal sources of sound, Catholic teaching. Use a question and answer from any Catholic show you like and mull it over in your journal.

## PRAYER CARDS AND PRAYER BOOKS

These are a bit different from devotionals. The prayer cards you find at a chapel or in the back of a church or at a shrine usually have special prayers printed on them, or they feature a saint who can intercede for a particular intention. Keep a supply of these cards nearby and grab one when you want to. There are also approximately one jillion Catholic prayer books that you can choose from. Find one that fits your season of life and your current needs, and you're all set to use it with your journaling.

## ALL THOSE BEAUTIFUL PRAYERS YOU MEMORIZED AS A CHILD—INCLUDING THE OUR FATHER AND HAIL MARY

Pull them out, dust them off, and really think about them. They have been created for our use and have been whispered by millions of Catholics over hundreds of years! Take them word-by-word and write a note or two on the meanings you find. In chapter thirty-six of the *United States Catholic Catechism for Adults*, The Lord's Prayer is called "the central prayer of Scripture" and is analyzed section by section.

## CATHOLIC ORGANIZATIONS

Boy, was it interesting to search for specifically Catholic groups on the Internet after I left my Protestant life. There are many, and they offer thought-provoking prayer journal resources. I still belong to some groups and receive their daily emails, while others I had to excuse myself from after I got to know them better. Like any other group, the Catholic Church has its continuum of members who range from unorthodox to orthodox. Keep your eyes wide open when you are looking for solid, faithful information from online groups. These groups can be a valuable resource of educational topics and encouragement, but they can also lead you astray if you're not careful. You can always ask your spiritual director or priest (or check in your new *Catechism*!) if you're not sure about the direction you are receiving.

## CLASSES AND BIBLE STUDIES

Your home parish or one nearby is bound to offer some classes or retreats or Bible studies throughout the year. If not, take a class online or order a series of DVDs on your own! Spending time with other Catholic Christians who want to learn more about the Bible and their faith will give you much to think about and write about. Don't feel intimidated or let your insecurity keep you away from these opportunities—chances are everyone else in the class is feeling a bit unsure of themselves too. Take a little hop of faith and get out there.

The Church has even more in her treasure chest for you. Take advantage of these options too:

**The liturgical seasons.** Grab special devotionals and daily prayer guides for Lent, Advent, and the Easter (for example, the Stations of the Cross), essays on the Holy Days of Obligation, and so on.

**The Divine Office or Liturgy of the Hours.** In case you are unaware (as I was), according to the USCCB, the Divine Office is "the daily prayer of the Church, marking the hours of each day and sanctifying the day with prayer. The Hours are a meditative dialogue on the mystery of Christ, using Scripture and prayer."[24] These prayers and homilies are not just for religious—they are also for the laity. Vatican II specifically wanted to make the Liturgy of the Hours available to everyone. You can find these prayers and more online at www.divineoffice.org.

**The Pope's lessons, encyclicals, and weekly audience topics.** There's even an app for that—The Pope App!

**Random stuff from the back of the church.** Not kidding here. I have picked up many interesting pamphlets, books, handouts, and fliers lying around in the front or back entryways, just begging for someone to grab them. Next time you're in that area of your church, take a gander and pick up something new to learn and use in your prayer journaling.

**The sacraments.** Especially reconciliation and the Eucharist—these are so rich with blessings for us. Journal about your last experience with confession—your thoughts before and after, the meaning of your penance, the feeling of absolution. What about the last time you received the Eucharist? How did you approach it? Think it through and journal your feelings about taking in the True Presence of Jesus—body and blood, soul and divinity. Your prayer journaling will be greatly enriched by Mass attendance and receiving the sacraments as often as you can. And vice versa!

This is a good starting list, wouldn't you say? Inspiration is everywhere, my Catholic friend. Even the back of the missalette found in the pew can be inspiring. I once read a prayer on the back cover that included the phrase, "Free us from seeking the easy answers." That made me gulp a little. *I think I seek the easy answers an awful lot,* I wrote in my prayer journal the next day.

These prompts and resources are critical in prayer journaling, especially when you're first starting out. Believe me, they'll lighten your load and help you exterminate the crickets and fill up those pages with ease. As a Catholic, you always have something to use to jump-start your writing, and these gifts are yours for the taking. The Church in her great wisdom has defined and passed down these tools and teachings for two thousand years, and they are free and accessible to everyone. They are yours to discover. They are yours to enjoy and integrate into your life. And they are yours to use as you prayer journal.

The Catholic Church has a treasure chest waiting for you. Open it!

One last thing—I have included a list of questions/prompts/conversation starters in the appendix of this book. Tear out the page (don't tell my publisher I said that), keep it near your journal, and pull it out whenever you're stalled. Easy peasy.

It's not cheating, honest.

<hr>

### COOL CATHOLIC QUOTE:

*"You don't know how to pray? Put yourself in the presence of God, and as soon as you have said: 'Lord, I don't know how to pray!' you can be sure you have already begun."*
*St. Josemaría Escrivá*[25]

## PRAYER JOURNALING PRACTICE

Which of the treasure chest prompts do you think you'd
like to try? Make a preliminary list in your journal,
based on the type of resources that seem to fit best with
your personality and interests.

Now, choose one from the list and begin using it.
Journal about the new treasures you discover and
the insights you gain from each one.

# *Six*

## A SPIRITUAL SHOPPING SPREE

*Rejoice always. Pray without ceasing. In all circumstances give thanks,
for this is the will of God for you in Christ Jesus.*
1 Thessalonians 5:16–18

My friends will attest to this fact: I am not a typical female who loves to shop. While I do appreciate a bargain, and I delight in finding the perfect gift for someone, I don't like spending time combing through racks of clothes, I don't enjoy endless traipsing from store to store, and I start to twitch if I have try on anything in a dressing room. I live in the sticks, many miles from a decent mall (and many miles from almost everything else), so it's a hassle to even get somewhere to shop. I'm usually an online shopper for those reasons. But there are times, even for me, when it's best to go shopping in a bricks-and-mortar store for an item I need, so I make the best of it. And there are times, unfortunately, when my husband ends up accompanying me. He does not like to go shopping with me. Even though I feel I am mostly a get-in-and-get-out type of shopper, my shopping habits are still far too "girly" for him. I'm not nearly as efficient as he is when shopping, and he tends to lose patience with me. "You go shopping," he says. "I go *buying*." So true.

But if *you* like shopping (at least more than I do), this may become your favorite chapter of the book.

For your spiritual shopping convenience, I am going to offer a variety of prayer patterns, processes, and formulas as well as informal methods of praying that you can learn and implement in your prayer journaling if you so desire. You get to view the selections, sift through the racks, check out the labels, and even try some on if you wish. Keep the things you want, the techniques that fit you well. Go back and get more of what you really like. Or return the method that didn't quite work out for you and move on to something different. You can take all the time you need to peruse—this shopping mall never closes! And I promise, there won't be anybody standing behind you tapping his impatient foot. You get to shop like a girl, not buy like a guy!

Keep in mind, my sister: I don't want you to get bogged down here, or feel like you want to run away screaming, the way I feel whenever I am overwhelmed with shopping options and hit the psychological shopping "wall." You don't need to learn all of these methods, or take them all in, or incorporate any of them at all. Prayer journaling is first and foremost prayer. And prayer can range from spontaneous, off-the-cuff, and free-flowing to a set formula. All formats are allowed—and *no* format is allowed! You can just as easily sit down and write to God without using any of these methods. Simply use this chapter (and the last one) as a reference—something you can turn to when you need a refresher or an injection of new life into your prayer journaling. It's hassle-free, no-obligation shopping!

Ready? Set? Shop!

## BLESSING AND ADORATION, PETITION, INTERCESSION, THANKSGIVING, AND PRAISE

The *Catechism* teaches us that there are five forms of prayer: Blessing and Adoration, Petition, Intercession, Thanksgiving, and Praise (*CCC*, 2625). You can incorporate each of these forms in your journaling for the day, or pick one a day and stretch it across a week.

Let's break them down a bit, shall we?

**Blessing and Adoration.** The *Catechism* describes blessing and adoration this way:

> *Blessing* expresses the basic movement of Christian prayer: it is an encounter between God and man. In blessing, God's gift and man's acceptance of it are united in dialogue with each other. The prayer of blessing is man's response to God's gifts: because God blesses, the human heart can in return bless the One who is the source of every blessing. (*CCC*, 2626)

> *Adoration* is the first attitude of man acknowledging that he is a creature before his Creator. . . . Adoration of the thrice-holy and sovereign God of love blends with humility and gives assurance to our supplications. (*CCC*, 2628)

When we offer blessings to God, we are responding to our own blessings! One of the blessings that prayer journaling has allowed me to respond to is the realization that God is always present in my life, as I noted one day: *Prayer journaling has helped me understand your constant presence. Not just every day as I journal, but every day, all day long. I don't have to call you or make an appointment or beg you to show. You are. . . . Always. The one thing in my life I can rely on. What a comfort and blessing to me!* When we adore him, we recognize his almighty power and his omnipotence; we acknowledge that he is our Creator. It puts our perspective where it needs to be.

**Petition.** One of the best ways to use your prayer journaling time is by asking questions, asking for forgiveness, and asking for help. God means it when he says we are to come to him with our requests. After all, we have been taught in Matthew 7:7, "Ask and it will be given you; seek and you will find; knock and it will be opened to you." Feel free to ask for God's help on all matters, big and small. He knows about them all, and he cares about them all, from the need to overcome an illness to the need for a parking space close to the school entrance when it's raining cats and dogs and you have your elderly mother-in-law in the car. Philippians 4:6 tells us, "Have no anxiety about anything, but in everything by prayer and supplication with thanksgiving let your requests be made known to God." *Everything*.

God even wants to hear us ask those rhetorical "Why me?" questions. I admit I have thrown that question at God every now and then in my journal. *Why am I afflicted with this condition? Why am I in this situation? Why didn't things work out the way I wanted them to?* Have no fear. He is used to these "why" questions; he will show you his love and give you strength to fight your battles.

Another one of my favorite questions to pose in my notebook is: *What would you like me to do, God? How can I fulfill the mission you have for me?* Over the span of several years, I've asked this question approximately fourteen thousand times. I was tired of being what I called a Spiritual Roomba. You know, one of those crazy little robotic vacuum cleaners that just goes and goes, bumping into furniture and changing directions every ten seconds? That's how I felt as I was trying to discern the next step in my faith life. *What about this? Or this? Or that? Should I be doing this, God?* God never lost patience with me, and eventually I found clarity (and eventually this book ended up in your hands!).

Notice I said I "eventually" found clarity? Don't be afraid to ask, but don't be surprised if the answers take a while to bubble to the surface. These are often deep queries, the kind we need to ponder for some time and then listen carefully for the answer. And what more perfect place than a prayer journal to work out such answers! I stink at waiting for answers from God (which is why I asked the Spiritual Roomba question so many times). But the act of writing down my questions for God was consoling in and of itself, and it helped me to grow in patience and trust and fortitude. And by looking back through my journals, I can see how my many questions were answered. Chalk up another benefit of prayer journaling!

If you're a mom like me, do you remember the toddler days when you were followed around the house by a two-year-old shadow, constantly asking "why" this and "why" that? And do you remember feeling a tad impatient after the umpteenth "why" of the day—how you just wanted to plop that child down in front of *Sesame Street* while you counted to ten and said a little prayer for more patience? It happened to me a lot. But here's some good news: God is not like us. He is never impatient with our questioning. In fact, he wants us to continue asking him questions! He is never tempted to turn on the TV and redirect us. He never has to count to ten. Unlike us, he has an eternal supply of love and mercy and forgiveness and patience for his children! Jesus instructed us to ask, so I ask away. You can too. Seek God and ask for his help and guidance and revelation in your life! Hang on to this verse: "Therefore I tell you, whatever you ask in prayer, believe that you receive it, and you will" (Mark 11:24). Ask for assistance and journal with him when you are faced with a life challenge. God does not want you to face your challenges alone.

**Intercession.** "I'll pray for you." Have you ever uttered those words to someone? Me too. Have you ever uttered those words and then forgotten to actually pray for them? Me too. As sincere as I am when I say it, I sometimes forget. That's where my prayer journal comes in handy. I keep a list on the back page of folks I want to lift up in prayer. I also make a note next to that person if I learn the outcome of the prayer—how it was answered or what new way I need to pray for them.

St. Paul tells us in Galatians 6:2, "Bear one another's burdens, and so fulfil the law of Christ." Praying for others is not only a command—it's an act of love. We know that it works. And when I pray for someone else, it gets my mind off my own troubles and turns it toward others. Intercessory prayer is a win-win! Pray for others every day, and use your prayer journal to make it happen.

**Thanksgiving.** The Church knows it's a wise practice to include thanksgiving in our day. And why not? In 1 Corinthians 4:7, St. Paul asks us: "What have you that you did not receive?" I can tell you that answer: N-O-T-H-I-N-G. Everything we have is a gift! What if we lived our lives with that full awareness? How would our behavior change? How would our attitude be different? As Catholic Christians, we believe God created us and is the One who blesses us with talents, virtues, charisms, abilities, and grace. We know we are to thank him for his goodness and the many gifts he bestows on us. We understand that thanking God and recognizing that he is responsible for our gifts is a pathway to joy and peace.

In addition to the profound spiritual, Christian reasons we should show our gratitude, research by the secular world has recognized the benefits of expressing daily gratitude as well. According to a multitude of studies, people who practice the habit of being thankful are more likely to:

- Sleep better
- Have less anxiety
- Gain better control of their tempers
- Have more energy
- Be more optimistic
- Handle tragedy and crisis better, and more!

That's a list of improvements I would welcome in my life! An increase in gratitude is a shortcut to joy. Ann Voskamp, author of *One Thousand Gifts*, challenged herself to write down one thousand gifts for which she was thankful. She discovered that this practice was the key to overcoming her depression and finding joy in her life. "Gratitude wins our wars," she concludes.[26] But this gratitude, this attitude of thankfulness, doesn't come naturally to most of us. We have to practice it to get good at it. And where is the perfect place to practice thankfulness? Of course—your new prayer journal. Start your day by listing three, five, ten things for which you are grateful. It will set a positive tone for the next twenty-four hours of your life. No matter which format you decide to use in your prayer journaling habit, be sure to include thank-you notes to God. It'll make his day—and yours!

**Praise.** Prayer journaling is a special time for us to praise God. Now I must admit, the idea of praising God beyond attending Mass, singing, and saying particular prayers initially had me a little stumped. How do we praise God, exactly? It was a good time for me to turn to the *Catechism* for advice:

> Praise is the form of prayer that recognizes most immediately that God is God. It lauds God for his own sake and gives him glory, quite beyond what he does, but simply because HE IS. (*CCC*, 2639)

I was making it too difficult. All I needed to do was be grateful to God that he is God! I just needed to remind myself, as my husband is fond of saying, "God is God, and I am not." Does God *need* to hear from us that he is a good God? Um, no. But he does want us to praise him because praising and worshipping him is for *our* benefit. It helps us grow closer to him as our Father. He is worthy of all our praise and honor. Tell him! Turn to the psalms (or the Liturgy of the Hours) if you need a little boost in this category, as I so often do. The psalms are filled with expressions of praise for God's pure goodness. For example, Psalm 145:3 tells us, "Great is the Lord, and greatly to be praised, and his greatness is unsearchable." Write that psalm in your journal and reread it with intention. Good job, my friend—you just praised God!

## HELP, THANKS, WOW, SORRY, YES

If I am rushed for time some mornings and don't have a particular subject to talk over with God, I use a quick method of prayer, one that is somewhat similar to the *Catechism's* recommendation. I learned it from author Anne Lamott, who wrote a book titled *Help Thanks Wow*. It encourages folks to pray three essential prayers:

1. "Help me, Lord!"
2. "Thanks, Jesus!"
3. "Wow, God!"

But because I can never leave well enough alone, I like to add two more words to that formula: "Sorry" and "Yes." I think "Sorry" is a useful addition because it reminds me of my need to repent (i.e., *There's no getting around it: I am a sinner*), and it also reminds me that Jesus is always ready and waiting to forgive me, no matter what I've done. I like tossing in "Yes" because, well, Jesus wants us to follow him and say yes to being his disciple. *Every. Single. Day.* Starting off my day by saying a simple "yes" to following Jesus helps me remember that my conversion is an ongoing work, and my surrender must be daily. Try using a "Help, Thanks, Wow, Sorry, Yes" formula yourself and see if it works for you.

## ACTS OR RAPT

When I started working in the healthcare field in the early 1990s, I soon was drowning in a sea of acronyms. It seemed like every term we used had to be reduced to a few letters! I had to figure out strange combinations like EGD, RRT, JCAHO, and HIPAA—and dozens more. I thought I would escape from acronym handcuffs when I moved to the financial industry, but no. There I was forced to contend with FDIC, CRA, and REO (unfortunately not the Speedwagon kind), and even a few they tried to make sound friendly with "names" like Fannie Mae and Freddie Mac (friendly they were not). But when it comes to prayer journaling, acronyms are helpful, and they won't be billed to your insurance or involve any late fees. You can use the ACTS method (Adoration, Contrition, Thanksgiving, and Supplication) or the RAPT method (Repentance, Adoration, Petition and Thanksgiving) to enhance your journaling. Both of these methods have been around for a long time, and can provide a focused way to pray. Search online for more information on these two options.

## MATTHEW KELLY'S PRAYER PROCESS

In his best-selling book *Four Signs of a Dynamic Catholic*, Matthew Kelly outlines a particular prayer process that could also easily be used with your prayer journaling. It involves seven steps:

- *Gratitude:* Begin by thanking God in a personal dialogue for whatever you are most grateful for today.
- *Awareness:* Revisit the times in the past twenty-four hours when you were and were not the-best-version-of-yourself. Talk to God about these situations and what you learned from them.
- *Significant moments:* Identify something you experienced today and explore what God might be trying to say to you through that event (or person).
- *Peace:* Ask God to forgive you for any wrong you have committed (against yourself, another person, or him), and ask him to fill you with a deep and abiding peace.
- *Freedom:* Speak with God about how he is inviting you to change your life, so you can experience the freedom to be the-best-version-of-yourself.
- *Others:* Lift up to God anyone you feel called to pray for today, asking God to bless and guide them.
- *Pray* the Our Father.[27]

All you need to do to make this work for prayer journaling is to write out the responses to these steps instead of (or after) saying them aloud.

## THE EXAMEN

Thanks to St. Ignatius of Loyola, we have another method of praying that can help us concentrate and cover all the bases, so to speak. Called the Daily Examen, it's a practice that teaches us to reflect on and "examine" the experiences of our daily life. It is usually conducted at noon and again at the end of our day, but you can easily work it into your morning prayer journaling routine as well. Simplified, it looks like this:

1. Place yourself in God's presence. Give thanks for God's great love for you.
2. Pray for the grace to understand how God is acting in your life.
3. Review your day—recall specific moments and your feelings at the time.
4. Reflect on what you did, said, or thought in those instances. Were you drawing closer to God or further away? Look toward tomorrow—think of how you might collaborate more effectively with God's plan. Be specific, and conclude with an Our Father.

When I think about it, the habit of prayer journaling can be one long handwritten Examen. Give it a try![28]

## LECTIO DIVINA

In a recent Bible study, I learned how to practice the art of Lectio Divina. Have you heard of it? *Lectio Divina* is Latin for "divine reading" or "spiritual reading" of Sacred Scripture. It's a form of slow, meditative prayer that focuses on listening and responding to God's Word. You can look it up online for more details, but basically it's an ancient tradition of the Church that can help us better encounter Jesus through what we read in the Bible. And it seems to be custom-made for prayer journalers. It consists of five steps: Invoke, Read, Meditate, Pray, and Contemplate.

- *Invoke:* Invite the Holy Spirit to guide your reading of Scripture.
- *Read:* Slowly read the Gospel passage for the day. Ask yourself: What stands out? What is the passage saying?
- *Meditate:* Sit with this passage for a moment. Read it again. What is God saying to you? Try to listen for his voice.
- *Pray:* Read the passage again and then focus on how you should respond to God. What do you want to say to him? Talk to him and open yourself to his will.
- *Contemplate:* Rest with God and listen closely with your heart. Think about how you can put into practice what he told you.

Wherever Lectio Divina asks you to meditate or talk with God, there's your chance to journal. I encourage you to learn more about this practice and decide if it is a tool you want to incorporate into your Bible reading and prayer journaling time. It has been very fruitful for me.

## EUCHARISTIC ADORATION

A prime example of getting benefit out of praising and worshipping God is through spending time in Eucharistic adoration.

Girlfriend, I am not overstating when I say establishing the habit of going to Eucharistic adoration accelerated my spiritual growth by leaps and bounds. It is a place like no other . . . and an encounter like no other. It has reinforced for me the deeply moving understanding of Jesus' constant and reassuring presence in my life—in all of our lives. I can see him on the altar, and I know—*I really know*—that Jesus is still here with us. He has not abandoned us, and he never will! Letting that concept sink into my soul over the course of an hour can humble me, lift my doubts, and infuse a fresh faith in my heart. So go ahead, try it. Take your prayer journal, or a different journal you can designate as your adoration journal, and just sit for thirty minutes to an hour in front of the exposed Blessed Sacrament. Jot down the thoughts that come to your mind or write nonstop—whatever feels comfortable to you. You can also use your journal during adoration as a Q&A session with God, pouring out your questions and being ready to hear his answers. Talk to God, praise him, thank him, and listen for his voice in the stillness of the chapel or church.

## USE YOUR BRAIN

Are you a left-brained, logical person who likes lists, spreadsheets, organizational charts, and academic discussion? Use that tendency to your advantage when you prayer journal. You may want to hunker down with the *Catechism*, grab a book on Catholic theology, or study a text on the history of the Church. You can also develop an ongoing prayer list (with answers received), a gratitude list, a list of your sins to take to confession, or a compilation of favorite new verses that spoke to you. Your prayer journaling method could be one ongoing list of bullet points if you want. Explore and find your own comfortable methods.

Are you a creative, right-brained type of person who is drawn to art, music, or poetry? Get out your colored pencils and draw in your journal. Play some hymns while you journal, or use a collection of Catholic artwork as stimulation for your writing. At the same Bible study where I learned the practice of Lectio Divina, the workbook we used featured magnificent artwork at the beginning of each chapter. I had never seen some of the creations before, and I was mesmerized by them. In particular, the painting of Mary at the Annunciation[29] captivated me. I had a very difficult time prying my eyes away from it and moving on to the lesson. If a piece of artwork strikes you that way, write about your reaction to it!

You can use your imagination to plop yourself right into the scene from the day's readings. St. Ignatius was fond of this method of imaginative prayer. It's an interesting way to "see" the people in the Bible passage, "hear" the words they speak, and observe how they act. What questions would you have? How would you describe the looks on people's faces? How would you react if you were hanging out with Jesus in that same scene? Record your thoughts in your journal.

Are you a nature lover? Me too! Sit outside or near a window when you do your prayer journaling. Or take your journal outdoors and soak up the sun while you write. Take a walk and stop along the way to write about the beauty and wonder of

God's creation. Love architecture? Photography? Your reaction to his creation is God-given. Give it back to him in your prayer journal. He will be delighted!

## TAKE IT OR LEAVE IT

There are countless other prayer journaling options for you to sample—these are only some of them. They are not to be considered the whole ball of wax and the authoritative say-so. But they should give you an idea of what's out there for your "how to pray with my prayer journal" shopping sprees. And again, you don't have to use any of them! There's no right or wrong way, no perfect approach that everyone has to utilize. You can stuff your shopping bag to overflowing, or you can exit the store empty-handed. Take it all or leave it all, my friend!

You're welcome, and thanks for shopping with me today! It was much more fun than shopping with my husband . . .

### COOL CATHOLIC QUOTE:

*"Acquire the habit of speaking to God as if you were alone with him, familiarly and with confidence and love, as to the dearest and most loving of friends."*
St. Alphonsus Liguori[30]

## PRAYER JOURNALING PRACTICE

Pick a prayer method from this chapter and run through
it in your journal. How did it flow? Is it something
you will continue to use?

Start on a blank page and list things you are grateful for
until you fill up the page. Did you find doing this difficult or
easy? Did anything surprise you about the list?

# Seven

## MORE TIPS, TRICKS, BOOSTS, AND HACKS

*When you call me, and come and pray to me, I will listen to you.*
*When you look for me, you will find me.*
Jeremiah 29:12–14

OK. Let's take a big, deep breath and review. We've covered the "whys" and the "hows" of prayer journaling. You know what the essentials are, and you know how to find resources, prayer formulas, and references that will help you. You could close this book right now and be ready and able to start a new prayer journaling habit with very little trouble. You have all the tools and practical instructions you need.

But wait—*there's more!*

I know it sounds a little like a late-night TV commercial for stain remover, but there really is more to know about successful prayer journaling. After many years of fine-tuning the habit, I have realized that just having a pen and a notebook and a place and time to write does not always produce the fruit I want. It's enough to get started, but it's not always enough to get the answers and direction we are seeking. It's as though we now have the car, and we've put gas in it, but we aren't quite sure where this thing is headed. We may need some extra coaching and some helpful hints to reach our destination in the most effective way. It reminds me of when my son had just turned sixteen and was trying to get from one city to another for his first basketball practice with a summer league (pre-GPS and map app technology). He had his car prepped with a full tank of gas, but once he headed into unfamiliar territory and knew his time was dwindling, he felt lost and unsure of himself. He didn't feel fully equipped for the journey. He was going nowhere fast. He called his dad and with great frustration he implored, "Dad, *where am I?*"

After a few clarifying questions (and more than a few laughs), my husband gave my son some advice on how to stay on track and get where he wanted to be in the most efficient manner. It was just the boost he needed to reach his ultimate destination.

There are ways to boost your prayer journaling adventure as well—ways to approach your journaling time that will make your experience a deeper and more satisfying endeavor. Have you ever tried to recreate a project you saw featured on Pinterest? For those of you who may be voluntarily or involuntarily living "off the grid" or have no access to the Internet, Pinterest is a an online idea playground where you can find just about any craft or building project on any subject you could ever want, with full instructions and pictures. (Confession: I may be addicted to Pinterest, and my husband may have muttered "Pinterest *again?*" more than once when he has caught sight of a new and unusual Pinterest project around the house). Well, Pinterest is full of projects labeled "hacks." Hacks are ways to take something standard and make it amazing. Buy a plastic basket at the dollar store and turn it into a lovely desktop organizer, or take a plain bookshelf and make it into a showpiece. Hacks can be shortcuts or ways to change something that is already acceptable in its own right into something you never imagined.

Let's have a look at a few prayer journaling tips, tricks, boosts, and hacks so you can take a good thing and make it great. You will develop your own boosters and hacks as you continue to grow in your prayer journaling, but these will get you revved up and in a good state of mind to begin your paper conversations with Jesus. They will speed up and multiply the rewards you receive from your efforts. And who doesn't want that?

## TIP/TRICK/BOOST/HACK (HEREAFTER REFERRED TO AS TTBH) #1: ACT LIKE A CHILD

First up on the list of tips, tricks, boosts, and hacks? You need to go back to being a child.

Yep, I'm telling you, a grown woman with kids and a mortgage and responsibilities, to take it down a notch. To take off your momma/grandma/all-around busy woman hat and go back to being that curious child you once were. A child who hoped. A child who trusted. A child who was full of expectations. A child bursting with questions, who was ready, willing, and able to learn. Childlike faith means cutting down our pride, becoming dependent, giving up control of our lives, and allowing Jesus to reign over us, guide us, and be our good shepherd. Empty your heart of suspicion, skepticism, cynicism, and doubt—all those characteristics we often develop as we grow older. Children don't exhibit those characteristics! When you have kicked those negative qualities to the curb, then your heart will be more open to the Lord's revelation and the Holy Spirit's wisdom. St. Thérèse of Lisieux teaches us the importance of becoming like a child:

> In our relationship with God we are very small children. We always will be. There is no need to be anything else. On the contrary it is essential that we never try to be anything else.[31]

When we become like children, we become teachable. Moldable. Empty vessels. We don't worry about feeling foolish and we don't hesitate to be real and honest with Jesus in our journals. In Matthew 18:3 Jesus said, "Amen I say to you, unless you turn and become like children, you will never enter the kingdom of heaven." We need to be listening to him, sitting at his feet, looking up at him and learning in wonder. We need to be curious about him and what he wants to tell us and teach us. Will we grasp it all? No. But we don't need to be hindered by the things we don't quite understand. One thing I've learned over the last few years through prayer journaling is that it's OK to view parts of our faith as a mystery and not have an answer to every question. What a relief that is! Many things we won't fully understand until we are finally sitting at Jesus' feet in heaven. Just trust and keep moving forward with childlike enthusiasm.

Here's a bit of terrific trivia to wrap up this section: The origin of the word *enthusiasm* is *en* plus *theos* in Greek, which basically means "inspired by God." If you sit down in your prayer chair with childlike enthusiasm, you will be inspired by God! Look for and expect great things from your prayer journaling, my friend, and great things will come.

## TTBH #2: GO ASK YOUR MOTHER!

I'll bet you have heard this phrase in your household more than once. But this time, you're off the hook. Here, I'm referring to our Holy Mother Mary. As I was studying the life of Mary and the act of consecrating our lives to Jesus through her, it hit me like a ton of bricks: Mary is the perfect model for how we Catholic women can approach our prayer journaling. Think about it: Mary was trusting. Mary was open to hearing the voice of God in her life. Mary's heart was "soft"—she was receptive and ready to say yes to God. Mary was not afraid. She asked questions, but then she pondered what she had heard and carried the beautiful revelations she received in her heart. And we can all be thankful that Mary yielded to God's plan for her life. Her "fiat" to God two millennia ago opened the door to our redeemed lives in Christ today!

The more I thought about the qualities Mary possessed, the more I realized I lacked them—big time. Mary is full of grace and trust and courage and a willingness to yield, and I, sadly, am not. But here's the good news: Mary stands ready to help us! She has a special role as the Mother of God and Queen of Heaven, and that is to help us find our way to Jesus. Let her! Ask her to soften your heart, help you ponder, and open your ears so that you may hear God speaking to you. She knows the drill; she can help! She will not let you down. Just take a look at these words from the beginning of the Memorare: "Remember, O most gracious Virgin Mary, that *never* [my emphasis] was it known that anyone who fled to thy protection, implored thy help, or sought thy intercession was left unaided."

Mary did not leave me unaided. I credit her for the softening of my heart that took place over the course of a year or so and was reflected in my prayer journal and in my life. Slowly but surely, she drew me nearer to Jesus and back to his Church. I didn't realize at the time that it was her intercession, but it eventually came as a Holy Whisper: *Wait. Was that you, Mary? It was you! It was you the whole time!* I know how much of a struggle that was, and what an accomplishment it is, and how grateful and humbled I am for her involvement, so I wear a blessed Miraculous Medal in her honor. It serves as a reminder of her influence in my life. If you battle self-sufficiency, independence, willfulness, pride, or lack of trust like I did (and still do), Mary could be your go-to prayer journaling partner.

And during those times in your life when you are being asked to do something that makes you shake in your boots, or that you do not want to do (even though you know in your heart it is the right thing), turn to Mary's wisdom. At the wedding feast at Cana, we hear her say some of the few words recorded in the Bible as hers, but which happen to be some of the most profound: "Do whatever he tells you." Kind of sums up the whole message of discipleship right there, doesn't it? When I was feeling a Holy Spirit elbow in my ribs to volunteer for a position that was way outside my comfort zone, I ignored it for a long time. But in the end, Mary's "Do whatever he tells you" won out, and I stepped up. And it worked out beautifully. Wise woman, our Mother. Seek her counsel in the pages of your journal.

## TTBH #3: LET THE SAINTS MARCH IN!

When our kids were nine and eleven, my hubby and I took them to the Grand Canyon. I had always wanted to hike a canyon trail, so one super-hot, sunny July afternoon, we grabbed a small backpack and stuffed it with a few water bottles and a couple of apples and granola bars and then took off down a trail. The hike we wanted to take was round-trip to and from the first shelter house on the trail, about three miles total, so I wasn't concerned. I regularly walked four to five miles a day at that time. How tough could it be?

Well, to make a long story short, by the time we had completed the first mile-and-a-half, we were sweaty, grouchy, and exhausted. We were out of water. And snacks. I was getting one of my infamous "I'm-a-fair-skinned-blonde-and-I'm-overheating" headaches. And my daughter had been nipped by a hungry, over-eager squirrel that had lunged for a piece of granola she was holding. When we finally arrived at the shelter house, we rested and refilled our water bottles, but we wondered how we would be able to summon the strength to make the return trip—going uphill this time.

Enter our own personal band of angels—the good folks along the (appropriately named) Bright Angel Trail who came to our rescue. They gave us more water, saltine crackers, walking sticks, and sunflower seeds. They encouraged us by telling us,

"You're almost there! You can do it!" They taught us how to tie wet bandanas around our necks to stay cooler. They guided us through the tricky narrow parts of the trail. And they cheered us on as we took the last few steps and snapped pictures of us, weary but triumphant, at the top of the trail. Someone even bought us ice cream at the lodge afterward!

In the Catholic Church the Communion of Saints is a lot like those fellow trail hikers in the Grand Canyon. The saints are our intercessors, our coaches, our fans along the path to the finish line. They go before us, and they walk beside us. They want to help you and pray for you from their seats of honor in heaven. Let them! Learn about them! Write about them! While compiling this book, I learned a great deal about St. Francis de Sales—how his character was so gentle and how he won many souls by practicing his own axiom, "A spoonful of honey attracts more flies than a barrelful of vinegar."[32] He is also said to have coined the term "Grow (bloom) where you are planted"—a personal favorite of mine and the meaning of which I have journaled about quite often, unaware that it was a quote generated by a saint! Reading about the saints or reading the writings of the saints can give you much fodder for your journal. You can even pick a Prayer Partner Saint—your baptism or confirmation saint, perhaps? What questions can you ask him or her? How can this saint help you along your trail?

## TTBH #4: LISTEN UP!
Do you remember participating in Christmas gift exchanges when you were in grade school? Everyone brought in a dollar

gift, wrapped and labeled either "For a Boy" or "For a Girl." Yes, it was fun to pick out a Matchbox car or a Bonne Bell Lip Smacker or a Life Saver candy "book" and give it to a classmate. But oh, the anticipation of receiving a gift was over the top! I could hardly wait to tear open the paper and see what marvelous surprise was inside.

Prayer journaling is similar to a gift exchange. We give our prayers and our thoughts and our questions to God, and we have the potential to receive many graces in return. But in order to be on the receiving end, we must stop and listen. We have to take time to unwrap the gift he gives to us. St. Teresa of Calcutta put it this way: "Prayer is putting oneself in the hands of God, at his disposition, and listening to His voice in the depth of our hearts."[33]

Listening is a critical skill that has fallen by the wayside in recent years. I know I'm often not very good at it. I have a bad habit of butting in and interrupting or just plain tuning out. I want to jump ahead in the conversation. But listening and paying attention is how we learn more about the other person in a relationship. It's how we fall in love. It's how we get feedback and how we realize just how much the other person loves us. And the only way we will know what the answer is after we have asked a question? By listening.

Sarah Young is familiar with this gift exchange. Author of the popular devotional book, *Jesus Calling: Enjoying Peace in His Presence*, she had been writing in her journal for many years, but realized that "this was one-way communication: I did all the talking." She began to wonder if she could change her prayer times "from monologue to dialogue." She decided to listen with pen in hand, writing down whatever she "heard" in her mind. "I was not listening for an audible voice; I was spending time seeking God's face," she relates. As a result, her practice of being still in God's presence increased her intimacy with him "more than any other spiritual discipline."[34]

Prayer journaler Diane has a beautiful way to describe this part of the process:

> I like to let Jesus take the pen. I write a prayer and then in another paragraph I let Jesus talk to me. I write what he is saying to me. It's amazing when I go back and read it how powerful his words are to me.

So go ahead and write, write, write when you sit down to prayer journal. But do remember to hand over your writing instrument and pause to listen as well. Let Jesus take your pen! Without this step, prayer journaling doesn't work. A gift exchange is no fun if you only get to give and don't have the opportunity to receive. It's one-sided. We need to give and receive, talk and listen. Pausing and listening and paying attention while prayer journaling will open you to a multitude of surprises and new understandings.

There you have it—some spiritual hacks that I have "pinned" on my prayer journaling board and offer to you. By being child-like, enlisting the help of Mary and the saints, and really pausing to listen for God's voice, we can boost our prayer journaling to an optimum level. Happy hacking, girlfriend!

### COOL CATHOLIC QUOTE:

*"If you listen, God will also speak to you,*
*for with the good Lord, you have to both speak and listen.*
*God always speaks to you when you approach*
*him plainly and simply."*
*from the Prayer of St. Catherine Laboure*

### PRAYER JOURNALING PRACTICE

What has Mary's role been in your faith journey? In your
prayer journal, reflect on an opportunity or challenge that
Mary can help you say "yes" to at this time in your life.

Do you have a favorite saint?
How can that saint help you with prayer journaling?
What saint would you like to learn more about?

# Eight

## THOSE TINY (AND NOT SO TINY) REVELATIONS

*And your ears shall hear a word behind you, saying, "This is the way, walk in it," when you would turn to the right or when you turn to the left.*
*Isaiah 30:21*

For as long as I can remember, I've been a doodler. When I was a senior in high school, my friend Nadine and I filled a six-foot section of a paper tablecloth with a host of (what we thought were) hilarious doodles and running commentary on the speeches at the athletic banquet we were attending. Our tablemates were impressed with our "artistry" and our "wit." It was so "epic," as high school standards go, that I tore out and kept that piece of tablecloth in my memory book. As an adult, I still doodle. I often fill the margins of my notepaper with comments and drawings out of painful boredom, like I did when I was forced to attend monthly meetings that covered the potential for the Federal Reserve Board to raise or lower interest rates (*zzzzzz*—sheer torture for me). Other times I doodle as I'm listening to a speaker and I want to illustrate, however poorly, an important concept I want to remember. But unless you count the five minutes of fame I received from the athletic banquet incident, my doodles were never very productive or helpful.

Until I started prayer journaling.

Suddenly the notes and symbols I was compelled to draw in the margins of my writing were significant. They marked times when I had a "lightbulb moment"—when the Holy Spirit opened my ears to a Holy Whisper, and I just had to highlight it somehow. Words are circled, asterisks are placed, happy arrows point to the tiny revelation I have just come across. Once in a while a sad face appears in the margin. But mostly I mark the newfound understanding with an energetic, joyful stroke of my pen. (Happy faces are encouraged, too—God likes to make us smile!)

When I received my first Holy Whisper in the form of a thought that just popped into my head "out of nowhere," I wrote down what I had just "heard." And then I circled it and underlined it and made an asterisk in the margin! I wanted to document and safeguard the valuable gem I had just received so I could come back to it later. This is the unique difference between traditional prayer and prayer journaling—you get to visually capture thoughts and notions and insights that you want to remember. Your Holy Whispers will be right there in black-and-white!

Keep in mind that Holy Whispers are not always in-your-face obvious. They are not "burning bushes." (Wouldn't it be nice if they were?) You have to be still and listen (see instruction in previous chapters) in order to notice them—they are "whispers," after all. They can sneak up on you in a variety of ways: Thoughts can "pop" into your head; you might feel a sudden surge of emotion like sadness, happiness, or anger. A solution to a problem materializes, or you finally understand something that has always confused you. A seed of an idea is planted. You feel a sense of peace and contentment or a fresh inspiration or desire arises in your heart. Be on the lookout! Holy Whispers are what set prayer journaling apart from mere journaling—you don't want to miss them.

Here are a few more examples of Holy Whispers I have marked in the pages of my prayer journal:

*Thanks for helping me through yesterday. You told me not to worry, so I didn't! One huge burden was lifted and another resolved successfully. Why don't I put these things in your hands more? Like every day? I dwell and stew and let mistakes and problems weigh me down. But when I offer it to you, I am freed. My perspective changes. You lighten my load. I need to remember this lesson—worry is a form of unbelief.*

*Surrender. That word just came after reading the Magnificat. Hey . . . maybe the two women with the strongest faith in the Bible, my namesakes, can help me surrender. Hmmm. Humble, joyful, pondering, faithful women doing difficult things in the name of obedience? Yeah, I could use their help. Help me, Mary and Elizabeth!*

*It's a pink-and-blue-sky morning. Lord, I don't know how music gets on a CD. Or how my phone works. Or how a car starts by using fossil fuel from deep underground. Or why the sky is pink and blue. Or why you love me. My car may not start and my phone will break and the sky may fall! But you will always love me. I can rest in that assurance.*

*This summer has been so difficult, Lord. I'm ready to run away. "Run to me. I am your refuge. I see what's happening. I know. I care. Rest in me. It IS hard. This is taking up your cross and following me. Stay focused on me. Take my hand. You are not alone."*

Notice the different ways the whispers come to me? They're a mix of thoughts, senses, new understandings, and consolation. I also get inspiration on what to discuss at the next book study at church, or a new blog post idea might surface:

*Lord, help me lift my eyes and fix them on you to get through this day. It's kinda like when my exercise instructor tells me to pick a spot on the wall to stare at when I feel like I'm losing my balance! (Hey, I should blog about that!)*

I often sense a "settled feeling" from my Bible reading:

*Nothing in here is random. You did nothing random in the Old Testament, and you did nothing random in the New Testament. There is deep purpose and meaning behind everything in your Word!*

And I cannot overestimate the number of times I have simply received a message of peace:

*OK, I get it. Keep pace with you. Don't move forward without you. If I take your hand, I will have peace. If I race ahead, I will have panic.*

Prayer journaler Adriene has experienced Holy Whispers too. "I love when I'm journaling my thoughts and prayers for the day, and then I'll read a devotional and a message of reassurance is given to me," she says. "I literally get chills just thinking about it." Diane has experienced them also. "I feel at peace when I get a nudge from the Holy Spirit showing me what I am meant to do," she explains. "I have definitely learned that if you listen, God will speak to you, even though sometimes it is not what you want to hear and it's hard to accept."

## HOLY MOLY MOMENTS

In addition to the Holy Whispers, you may also receive louder messages. I call them Holy Moly Moments. I've had a few of those over the years. Holy Moly Moments go beyond the tiny revelations of insight and understanding—they can be full-on shouts in your head! They are thunderclaps and lightning strikes and inspiration landslides that make you blink or wince or sit back in your chair and say, "Whoa!" They are times of conviction or stark realizations. They can make you laugh out loud or shed a few tears or jump up and dance.

I had all three reactions to one particular Holy Moly Moment—my favorite one of all time. It's what I call My Holy Moly Moment of True Conversion. It was March 2014 and I was writing in my journal at 7:10 a.m. It was Lent, and the previous day I had gone to my first "real" sacrament of reconciliation since my official return to the Church almost a year prior. (A little backstory: before returning to Catholicism, I had a meeting with our priest about the process and he guided me through a reconciliation so I could receive the Eucharist the following Sunday. I hadn't been to traditional confession since then. Let's face it—I was too chicken.) Here's what the entry looked like that morning:

*So. I finally get to sit and process my reconciliation experience from 4:00 yesterday. Prodded myself to go—had no idea what to expect. Seven priests—who would I get? How would he react to me and my first official confession and my return to the Church?*

*I want to remember it forever. Forever!*

*I felt like the prodigal daughter being welcomed home by the Father. The priest was Jesus. I felt his love and excitement and interest and joy. I have goosebumps! "Exuberant" was his word. I think if there was no curtain between us he would have jumped through and hugged me. As it was, I watched his big black shoes move back and forth excitedly (and I could see that because the light was on in there—whaaa? They have lights on in there now?). He asked me how I was doing now. He spoke of the joy that heaven has because I am back. He encouraged me to continue to take baby steps and to fully experience the mercy, peace, and joy of Christ and his Church.*

*Thank you for being in the confessional with me. He loved me. You loved me. He was overjoyed at the lost sheep coming back. I know now that you must be too! What a beautiful gift that is to proud, independent me. That I am a much-loved child of yours. You love me. I forgot, or didn't think about your joy of my return—only mine. You missed me! You left the ninety-nine to come and get me. You are exuberant!*

*Reconciliation.*

*God knows who I am and he had felt my absence. Whoa. He knows ME. He loves ME. ME.*

I forget how long I just sat in my prayer chair, choked with tears, and tried to absorb the grace of that moment. It was a long time. And I did not want it to end. Two days later my journal showed that I was still glowing:

> *I know how happy I was to be back; I did not realize the magnitude of joy Jesus has that I am back. I am so loved. It never dawned on me like that. What a gift this is to me! I felt like it was a real, close encounter with Jesus.*
>
> *Because it was. He knows me. Wow. I am almost fifty years old before I really felt that strong of a connection. THIS is what conversion feels like. You know me. And you have plans for me. I have new life. New perspective. I am home.*

Let me tell you, there were many circles, asterisks, underlines, and exclamation points across those couple of pages! Part of the reason I am so biased about prayer journaling is because of this experience. Jesus drew me closer and closer and nearer and nearer until finally I fully felt it—the immensity of his personal love for me. How much he cares for me and about me; how he wants a relationship with me that's deep and authentic and meaningful. And guess what? He wants the same for you. The close encounters with Jesus are not just for me—they are available to you. He knows who you are and will leave the ninety-nine for you too! He wants to have a personal relationship with *you*! Holy Moly!

Debbie recounts one of her Holy Moly Moments: "I had a moment during prayer journaling when I realized that God the Father had been with me in a time of my childhood that was particularly difficult. I suddenly realized, 'That was you! You were there! It was you!' And he revealed this to me exactly when I needed it."

The big moments are not always cause for celebration, however. There was the time I realized the theme word I had picked for the New Year, "yield," did not mean what I thought it was going to mean. I was ready for a year of an avid, "bearing fruit" kind of yield. I was ready to get out there and do something with my new fiery faith. But what I learned instead that year was the humble, "surrender" kind of yield. The yield that makes you drop to your knees and cry out for help and say, "I give!" Yep, that was a biggie. It was all about accepting God's will in a family situation instead of trying to impose mine. I (eventually) realized I needed to yield/surrender *to* him before I could ever have a chance to yield/bear fruit *for* him. And my most recent Holy Moly Moment, which occurred while I was mired in an extended pity party for myself, involved a huge, bonk-on-the-head realization that *my wounds are self-inflicted*. Ouch. I had felt as if I was being punished anew for a past decision. But over time, through much prayer journaling, God showed me the difference between a self-inflicted, self-centered wound and a sanctifying sacrifice. He offered this understanding:

> *This is not a "wound"; it is a sacrifice. The sacrifice will bring you closer to me. It is ongoing, yes. But I promise it will not always bring you sadness. This sacrifice also brings joy. And I promise to always walk with you in the sacrifice.*

It's just amazing stuff, friend. Whether joyful or convicting, these Holy Moly Moments were turning points in my faith life. I am so grateful for them, and so humbled by the experiences. But just a word of caution: Don't let my excitement over Holy Whispers and Holy Moly Moments received in prayer journaling give you the impression that I have these experiences all the time, every day, and with the same constant pace that dirty laundry piles up in the laundry room. I don't. The examples I've shared in this book have come to me over the course of many years. I am not a mystic or a saint or even someone who feels extra close to God all day, every day. I am a passenger on the struggle bus, just like you. I am someone who has gotten much better at being quiet and listening, thanks to prayer journaling—but I have a long way to go. In fact, most of the time when I figure out something significant, I want to shake my head and say, *Duh, Mary Beth! How could you have not realized this before?* And I often go days or weeks without feeling that I'm making any progress at all. But that's another reason to prayer journal and mark your "moments"—when you feel like you are going through a time of spiritual dryness, you can open your past notebooks and smile and have renewed hope and faith. You will know that you are drawing nearer to Jesus, daughter of a King, one page at a time.

And another word of caution: If you are unsure about the meaning of a whisper or nudge or feeling or understanding, or even a Holy Moly Moment, be sure to reach out to a spiritual advisor or priest to help you discern. Four ears are better than two!

## YOUR UNIQUE MOMENTS

St. Augustine is often quoted as having said, "God loves each of us as if there was only one of us." This means the Holy Whispers you receive will be different from my Holy Whispers, and your Holy Moly Moments will be different from my Holy Moly Moments. God will speak to you in your own language. "If I sense something from the Lord, I write that down," says Debbie Guardino. "The more you pray, the more comfortable you are in knowing whether it's the Lord's voice you hear. The Lord is never speaking above my head in prayer journaling."

You will want to track those unique-to-you whispers and moments so you will be able to appreciate your steady spiritual growth and progress. I had always known that God's hand was at work in my life, but when I began to track my spiritual growth and insights through my journal pages, I was floored. I could clearly see that grace was changing me, that prayers were indeed answered, that I felt greater peace despite any upheaval that was going on in my life at the time.

Prayer journaling will help you see what God is doing in your life, too, if you learn to mark your moments. Adriene, Jackie, and Debbie have all seen the benefits of tracking and reviewing their journal entries. "It is so wonderful to look back at past entries—I can see just what God was showing me during all seasons of my life," said Adriene. "One of the best things about journaling is that it allows me to trace God's hand of faithfulness," Jackie said. "When I feel like God isn't hearing me, I can go back in my journal and see where God has been faithful even though he didn't answer my prayers like *I thought* they should be answered (*why* do we think we know better than

God?)." Debbie adds, "I rely on looking back on my previous prayer journaling experiences when things are difficult: *You did hear me and you answered!*"

Don't make your tracking method complicated. Doodle, circle, underline, and asterisk like I do. Or buy some of those cute mini sticky notes and tab your "Aha!" pages. Or, when you've almost completed a notebook, use the last couple of pages to summarize the things you've learned in that notebook. Ask yourself questions like:

- What have I discovered?
- Do I have a fresh perspective on an old problem?
- Do I have more clarity on my mission or vocation?
- Has my behavior changed in any way?
- What prayers have been answered and how?
- Is there a particular verse or quote that spoke to me?
- Do I have less desire to wring the necks of people that annoy me? (This is a thing. I know.)

If you really want to go all out, you can even keep a separate notebook to track your tiny and not-so-tiny revelations. It doesn't matter which method you choose, just pick one. You'll be glad you did. Remembering and being grateful for the good things God has done for you is essential to growth in your spiritual life. It is one of the main rewards of this new habit. Make sure you flag them.

I thank God for teaching me how to prayer journal and for allowing me to learn to listen and to feel his love and mercy through a mere pen and notebook. It's ridiculous, really. And miraculous! The more we come to God in prayer and prayer journaling, the more we will recognize his voice, his whispers, and even his shouts. They will be like sparks in your soul and you will learn to love them and crave them even more. This journal entry of mine in 2016 sums up the feeling:

> *Have I mentioned how I love this time with you? So mysterious, so blessed, so sacred, so personal. If my house was on fire and all the people were safe (and Sammy too, of course) I would go back in for these notebooks! They are that precious to me.*

## COOL CATHOLIC QUOTE:

*"We have to offer ourselves as pencils. Let him write poetry.*
*Let him write prose. Let him scribble.*
*What difference does it make? This is happiness."*
*Archbishop Fulton Sheen*[35]

## PRAYER JOURNALING PRACTICE

Have you ever "heard" a Holy Whisper? Describe it in your prayer journal—and write about how it affected you.

In what ways does Jesus speak to you most often?
List these in your journal.

# Nine

## GOOD BYE, CATHOLIC COUCH POTATO

*I know your works: you are neither cold nor hot. Would that you were
cold or hot! So, because you are lukewarm, and neither cold nor hot,
I will spew you out of my mouth.*
*Revelation 3:15-16*

There are a few quirky things about me that only my husband
knows (until now). One, I don't like cherry-flavored anything.
Two, I hate bats with every fiber of my being. (*Why, God? Why
create a creepy flying mouse that sucks blood?*) And three, I will not,
I repeat *not*, ever knowingly put my hands in dishwater that is
lukewarm. Yuck! Give me hot sudsy water, or even cold water,
but please, nothing in between. It gives me the willies for some
reason.

Jesus was not fond of lukewarmness either, but for a more
important reason. He wants believers to be on fire for their
faith. He wants us to be "hot." He wants us to look and sound
and act like our lives have been transformed by his love and his
grace and his message of salvation. He doesn't want us to be
lukewarm Catholics or lukewarm disciples—people who claim
to know him but whose actions leave others wondering. He

wants us to go all in! He doesn't want us to be complacent, spiritual couch-potatoes—those are the ones he promises to "spew" of his mouth!

## TURN UP THE HEAT

Those "lukewarm/spew you out" verses hinted to me rather strongly that Jesus wasn't kidding around. When I really pondered these verses a few years ago in my prayer journal, his words motivated me. I faced the uncomfortable truth: I had been spiritually sleepwalking for many years. I was not awake to how much Jesus loves me, and how much he wants me to be an evangelist for him. I was that spiritual couch potato, sitting around eating Doritos and flipping channels, thinking I was doing just fine as a sedentary Christian. I was going to church, trying not to break any commandments, being a "good" person. But I was not aware that my actions as a disciple of Jesus Christ were lukewarm at best.

I decided I had better ask for help in this area. I prayed to be cognizant of my lukewarm attitudes and responses, and to develop the courage to make them hot instead. And what I realized, after much journaling, was how I had kept Jesus at "arm's length" and how that in turn caused me to love others at arm's length. Being lukewarm and indifferent and "arm's length" is a personal weakness of mine, so overcoming it will be a lifelong process, I fear. But nothing put me on the fast track to becoming a "hot" Christian more than prayer journaling. It gave me a heightened sense of awareness, and instilled in me new courage and confidence to turn up the heat of my faith life. I began to do things I had previously never considered, like praying for my husband every day, offering to facilitate book studies at church

- Sunday school
- continue daily journal *Praying with a Pen* | **109**
  and bible reading
- get involved - do things for others.

and writing life stories for hospice patients and their families.
The deeper I fell in love with Jesus, the deeper I fell in love with
his other children!

Do not be surprised then, dear sister, when all your Holy
Whispers and your close prayer journaling encounters with
Jesus morph into kindling for a hot spiritual fire in you too!
When you begin to look back in awe at all the insight you have
gained from your prayer journaling experience, it will be nearly
impossible to leave that fire smoldering between the pages of
your notebook. You will be nudged by the Holy Spirit, quite
strongly at times, to act on all those insights.

Who knows what form your actions will take? Jesus knows,
as it has always been part of his plan for you. But *we* almost
never know where our newfound understanding will take us.
We just have to trust that we are supposed to make a change,
do something different, be open to a new way. We are asked to
step out in faith. And we have to believe that God will show us
how to do it, and give us the provision we need to accomplish
his work. He did not pursue you (or me) just to leave us alone!
It's that transformation thing he's after. And prayer journaling
will be the express route he takes.

Your discipleship action doesn't have to be something big
and newsworthy like starting an orphanage in Haiti (although
that would be cool). St. Teresa of Calcutta warns us against
grandiose notions that can sometimes thwart our good intentions: "Not all of us can do great things. But we can do small
things with great love."[36] In other words, there is much to be
done in our own backyards, in our own churches, in our own
communities. "Stay where you are. Find your own Calcutta,"

St. Teresa says.[37] If you're not sure about the direction you are receiving, seek counsel. Ask your priest or spiritual advisor or friends from church to help you discern. But know that God has something unique in mind just for you. Ask him to show it to you, and then stand back and watch the flames ignite. St. Catherine of Siena teaches us, "Be who God meant you to be and you will set the world on fire."[38]

When I asked God what I should be doing as a "hot" disciple during a prayer journaling time in Eucharistic adoration, I heard this answer in my heart almost instantly: *Watch and see what I place in front of you.* In other words, relax. He has a plan, and I can't force it. It's a process. As we become more aware of God in our lives, and God's hand in our lives, we will also become more aware of the opportunities in front of us to do his work and help build his kingdom. As he opens our eyes to himself, he will also open our eyes to others in need. As we grow in love for him, he will help us grow in love for others. According to Pope Francis:

> Scripture tells us: defend the oppressed, take care of your neighbor, the sick, the poor, the needy, the ignorant. This is the touchstone. Hypocrites cannot do this, for they are so full of themselves that they are blind to seeing each other. But when one journeys a little and draws near to the Lord, the light of the Father enables one to see these things and to go out to help one's brothers and sisters.[39]

He will shine a light. Watch and see what he places in front of you!

## DROP YOUR NETS

In Matthew 4:18–19, Jesus is beginning his ministry on earth and is looking for a few good men to join him: "As he walked by the Sea of Galilee, he saw two brothers, Simon who is called Peter and Andrew his brother, casting a net into the sea; for they were fishermen. And he said to them, 'Follow me and I will make you fishers of men.'" And how did they respond? Immediately they stopped what they were doing: "Immediately they left their nets and followed him" (verse 20). They dropped their nets, the very representation of their present lives, and they followed him. They heard the voice of Jesus and *obeyed*. The passage continues:

> And going on from there he saw two other brothers, James the son of Zebedee and John his brother in the boat with Zebedee their father, mending their nets, and he called them. Immediately they left the boat and their father, and followed him. (Matthew 4:21–22)

They too heard the voice of Jesus and *obeyed*.

I love the image of dropping our nets and following Jesus. It so aptly symbolizes a major transformation. It's a deliberate action that shows we are now doing something different. We are leaving the old life behind and learning to be true, non-lukewarm disciples of Jesus Christ. We are obeying and trusting and heading in a distinctly new direction. And we are following the best leader ever.

This is one crazy world we live in, girlfriend, and it's getting crazier by the minute. However, even though we may feel like we are helplessly spiraling downward as a society, we can do something about it. We can drop our nets. We can be different. We can respond to the hurt in this world with love. And kindness. And mercy. And service. Don't be a spiritual couch potato and watch like a snacking spectator as everything spins out of control. Be bold. Take what you are learning through prayer journaling and be the antidote to this cold, secular world. Catholic teaching holds that we will be judged on our faith *and* our works. You were born and you are here today for such a time as this!

## THE RIGHT PATH

My friend, it's time to get out of the Catholic baby pool. (Another witty message I "heard" while prayer journaling during adoration. God sure likes to use language I can easily relate to!) Life is short here on earth; we can't afford to be lukewarm any longer. Go forth. Drop your nets. When you decide to ditch the lukewarm and strive for hot, it's a sign that your prayer journaling is working and you are on the right path. It's a natural progression. As St. Teresa of Calcutta said, "If we pray, we will believe. If we believe, we will love. If we love, we will serve."[40] We will find it nearly impossible to keep our light under the bushel basket—we are compelled to let it shine. The whole purpose of prayer journaling and getting to know, love, and serve God this way is so that you can know, love, and serve others. Don't sit back—put up your dukes and go down serving!

A few years ago, I worked with our local hospice organization to interview the World War II veterans from our county about their experiences before, during, and after the war. The process took four days and we videotaped for over twelve hours but

I learned this fact in the first few minutes: Not one of those men was a lukewarm soldier! They knew what the right thing to do was and they did it without hesitation. I was awestruck by how they dropped their nets—by their sense of duty and commitment, their unquestioning obedience and their incredible sacrifice. It occurred to me that these men symbolize what a spiritual soldier should be, how a follower of Christ should be. We are not promised an easy path, or even a clear one. But we are commanded to follow and we are promised an eternal reward. As John 10:27 reveals, "My sheep hear my voice, and I know them, and they follow me."

My dear sister: Don't leave your tiny revelations on the page, where they will fade over time. You are the hands and feet of the Church. It's up to you to do something with your newfound inspiration and strengthened faith. St. Teresa of Avila tells us: "Christ has no body now but yours. No hands, no feet on earth but yours." Jesus needs you to help build his kingdom, friend. He will show you how. Drain that lukewarm-ness. Jump off that couch. Hear his voice, drop your nets, and follow!

### COOL CATHOLIC QUOTE:

*"God wants you to be in the world, but so different from the world that you will change it. Get cracking."*
*Mother Angelica, foundress of EWTN Global*
*Catholic Television Network[41]*

## PRAYER JOURNALING PRACTICE

Take some time to journal about where you see
Jesus calling you to let your light shine more brightly.

What holds you back from fully following him?
Pray about this in your journal.

# Ten

## REAL REST

*"Come to me, all who labor and are heavy laden, and I will give you rest."*
*Matthew 11:28*

If you're a parent, you have probably gazed at your children some days and seen nothing but God's amazing work, especially when they're fast asleep and looking all innocent and not getting into trouble! You stare at them and you see little miracles that you somehow incredibly had a role in creating. Though not nearly the blessing a child is, this is how you will come to refer to your prayer journaling—a little miracle that you get to participate in every day. It can become the doorway to your deep, personal relationship with Jesus. And it will become your source of wonder, peace, hope, mercy—and rest. Yep, your new prayer journaling commitment is a miracle in the making.

Part of the miracle lies in the fact that you, busy woman, have slowed down your pace in order to prayer journal. You have pressed the pause button on your life, and you are spending time with your Creator, the master of the universe, the one who loves you more than you can begin to imagine. You decided to put first things first and start your ordinary day in the most extraordinary way possible. You've set aside your daily distractions and responsibilities and you are meeting with Jesus. And does that ever thrill him! He's been relentlessly calling you to come and rest in him, and you answered him! Congratulations—by designating spiritual white space in your day, you have made room for many more miracles to flow in. And flow they will!

You will notice changes in a relatively short period of time. These changes won't necessarily be the ones you expect. You may not see answered prayers, or a clear direction, or even a better understanding of your faith (at least not at first). But if you persist in meeting with Jesus every morning and prayer journaling with him, you will not be disappointed. In my case, the biggest transformation happened in my heart. I did *not* expect that. Think of Dr. Seuss's Grinch, whose cold little heart grew and grew and finally burst through the frame that held it in place. That's how I feel when I think about how much my perspective has shifted over the years I have been prayer journaling. The Holy Spirit reached through the pages of my prayer journal and converted my stony, self-sufficient heart. I went from someone who kept my (weak) spiritual life private and separate from the rest of my life to someone who talks (out loud!) about her faith. I went from someone who kept saying "Prove it!" to God, to someone who regularly smiles and says previously-unheard-of-stuff like "Jesus, I trust in you." I now care much less about all the material things of the world; I'm more generous with my time, talents, and treasures; and I'm more forgiving than the person I was before I began prayer journaling. I still have a long way to go, but I'm calling this amount of progress an unquestionable miracle! Now it's your turn.

## TREAT YOURSELF

I love cookies, especially ones with chocolate chips. I would move mountains for a double chocolate chip cookie straight from the oven. And there's no telling what I would do for one with macadamia nuts added. Chocolate is incentive for me. If I know there's a chocolate chip cookie waiting for me when I have completed a deadline, you can be sure that deadline will be met. Chocolate is a reward.

I think of my prayer journaling as a reward too. It is my special, private time with Jesus that I crave. It is chocolate for my soul—and for your soul as well—with no calories! If you view your prayer journaling time as a reward for yourself, you will be more likely to start it, continue it, and see results from it. Partake as much as you want, girlfriend, and reap the sweet benefits.

## PROTECT THIS

My last bit of advice to you before you close this book? Do everything in your power to protect your rest time, your miracle-creating time, your chocolate-for-your-soul time, from the pressures of the outside world.

Did you notice how often I have mentioned something such as "today's society will not want you to do this . . . the current culture is opposed to stillness . . . it's difficult in our world to focus on Jesus"? That's because, dear friend, like Catholicism in general, prayer journaling in particular is countercultural, and you will be pressured to abandon it.

As a Catholic, you are used to going against the grain, so to speak. To be a practicing Catholic nowadays is to be brave, audacious, radical. We don't believe what the culture tells us to believe about abortion, euthanasia, or social justice. We believe in the sanctity of life from conception to natural death, the definition of marriage as between one man and one woman, and a loving God who created us in his image and likeness. Our values and doctrines and traditions are ageless and timeless. They've been around for more than two thousand years! They don't cave in to the most recent social trend, or get voted out and replaced with "modern" versions, as happens in so many other churches. It's one of the things I love the most about the Catholic faith—it is unchanging in a constantly changing world. And, in order to be faithful Catholics, we need to daily submit to the authority of our God and the authority of our faith. Submitting to any authority, much less a sacred, "religious" authority, is definitely frowned upon today. It's not "normal" in our self-centered, "it's all about me" environment.

Starting an "unusual" habit like prayer journaling will be viewed by many as strange as well. You'll get quizzical looks, awkward questions, and maybe some downright persecution. When I first talked about writing this book, I got this question from a close family member: "What are you, a *super* Catholic now?" Be prepared! But also know that God has your back on this. The more faithful you are, the more you will see his hand of protection and strength when it comes to fighting the battles

against "normal." Be not afraid! This is the command most re-
peated in the Bible. Be not normal, either, sister. Normal is dull
and boring, as I've told my kids since they were little. Normal
is an empty rowboat drifting on still water. It's un-flashy, non-
controversial, safe. It makes no waves and allows any old breeze
to carry it to any old destination. Don't be carried along by
society's waves. Instead, as Dynamic Catholic's tagline reminds
us: *Be Bold. Be Catholic.* And while you're at it—Be a Catholic
Prayer Journaler.

## REST IN HIM

When I was working at a downtown office, I would sneak away
on my lunch hour three times a week to attend an exercise class
across the street. I told people it was because the instructor was
excellent, the facility was great, and the workout was worthwhile. But what I really cherished were the last ten minutes
of the session. That's when the lights dimmed, the soft music
played, and the instructor let us lie there and drift off into heav-
enly oblivion. Many times I fell asleep. And yeah, I jerk-snorted
awake a time or two, truth be told. But I didn't care—I so needed that rest time.

As much as I enjoyed that break in the middle of my day,
it was nothing compared to the glorious rest time I get with
prayer journaling. Prayer journaling is the perfect rest: a time
to physically rest, a time to mentally rest, and a time to rest in
him. And that's exactly the way he prescribes it for his children. When the apostles returned from one of their first mission trips, Jesus's first concern was not about getting updates on

their work; he wanted them to catch their breath before facing the crowds again. He said to them, "Come away by yourselves to a lonely place, and rest a while" (Mark 6:31). Beyond what society wants to label as necessary "me time" for us hardworking women, this time is much more precious. It's "us time"— you resting in the arms of your God.

In this book you've read about many options you can use when you prayer journal. You sifted through a number of prayer methods, multiple resources available from the Church, and different ways to enhance your experience. You learned the importance of silence and designating a specific time to meet with God. And you know how critical it is to not just talk, but to listen and obey the voice of God. You are armed and ready for this adventure, girlfriend! But not one word in this book will be meaningful if you don't remember that your prayer journaling experience is deeply personal. It all boils down to just you drawing nearer to God. That's really it. It's that simple, that beautiful, that miraculous. It's nothing to take lightly! As this quote attributed to St. Augustine reminds us, "To fall in love with God is the greatest romance, to seek him the greatest adventure, to find him the greatest achievement."

## I DARE YOU

Every once in a while, I like a good dare. It gets me out of my routine and compels me to try something new. Prayer journaling against the pressures of the culture is a good dare. Try it. Stay with it. Let the Holy Spirit come alive and take up full-time residence in your heart. Find out what God wants you to discover about him. Let Jesus show you how much he loves you, his priceless, beloved daughter.

Seek Him. Find Him. Rest in Him. Go pray with a pen.

My closing prayer for you, my new Catholic friend, is that you feel the Lord himself greet you every morning as you devote time to him and press your pen to paper. May you find an upsurge of peace through your new prayer journaling habit. May your writing grant you clarity in purpose and help you develop an overwhelming sense of gratitude for the many blessings bestowed on you. May you speak to and listen to the Holy Spirit and be renewed by his strength and encouragement. I pray that the words in your notebook inspire you to live as who you are—a beloved daughter of the King. When you put down your pen, let your burdens be lightened, your prayers be answered, and your worries be erased. May you feel the deep, personal love God has for you. My friend, I pray you can look ahead in faith, with holy confidence and unwavering trust that God is by your side in every battle. May you drop your nets and help build the kingdom as only you are destined to do. And may you share your prayer journaling success stories with all of your Catholic girlfriends so they can draw nearer too.

God bless you on your holy adventure!

### COOL CATHOLIC QUOTE:

I thought it fitting to end our prayer journaling lessons the way we began—with some wise words from that patron saint of journalists and writers, St. Francis de Sales. This thought of his beautifully summarizes the prayer journaling experience:

*Sometimes of course, when we enter into God's presence we will not find ourselves speechless. We will be ready to speak to him and to hear what he has to say to us. Usually he will respond in quiet inspirations and in the silent movement of our heart. His voice will fill our souls with consolation and courage. So if you are able to speak to the Lord, do it with words of prayer. Praise him. Listen to him. But, if no matter how full your heart is with things you wish to say to God, your voice still fails you, stay right where you are in his presence. He will see you there, and bless your silence. And perhaps he will reach down and take you by the hand, walking with you, chatting with you, leading you gently through the garden of his love. Whatever happens, it is a great grace.*[42]

### PRAYER JOURNALING PRACTICE

What do you anticipate the rewards of your new prayer journaling habit will be? List them! (And then at the end of your list, give yourself a gold star from me!)

# Appendix

## FORTY PRAYER JOURNAL QUESTIONS/PROMPTS/ CONVERSATION STARTERS

- Jesus, I don't understand . . .
- God, yesterday was . . .
- Thank you, Lord, for . . .
- Dear Jesus, I am sorry for . . .
- God, help me to forgive . . .
- I want to follow you, but . . .
- At Mass the other day I was wondering . . .
- The burden I am carrying right now is . . .
- Lord, I need help with . . .
- I am afraid of . . .
- I have grown in _____, but I have made little progress in . . .
- I thought of you today when . . .
- My gifts and talents from you are . . .
- How can I be better at . . .
- I am really struggling with . . .

- The cross I don't like carrying is . . .
- I messed up, Lord. I . . .
- I love it when . . .
- I've always wanted to ask you . . .
- I am anxious about . . .
- How do I handle . . .
- The sin I commit the most is . . .
- I feel so blessed because . . .
- Lord, can you please show me . . .
- Am I on the right path if . . .
- What do I do next?
- Lord, please send me . . .
- Holy Spirit, inspire me to . . .
- Jesus, please teach me how . . .
- I know you know this, but . . .
- Lord, my children are . . .
- God, this world . . .
- Jesus, I ask for the virtue of . . .
- Where are you, Lord?
- Jesus, I'm so tired of . . .
- Was that your voice I heard when . . .
- I'm so excited when you . . .
- Jesus, I always thought . . . but now I know . . .
- God, I know I'm lukewarm about . . .
- Jesus, today I want to . . .

# ENDNOTES

1. Julia Cameron, *The Artist's Way: A Spiritual Path to Higher Creativity* (New York: Jeremy P. Tarcher/Putnam, 1992).
2. St. John Paul II, Mass with Youth, Czech Republic, 1997.
3. Purcell, M. 2016. "The Health Benefits of Journaling." Psych Central. Retrieved on April 29, 2017, from https://psychcentral.com/lib/the-health-benefits-of-journaling/.
4. Interview with Debbie Guardino, speaker, writer, blogger, and executive director of the Diocese of Trenton Catholic Charismatic Renewal in New Jersey; 10/4/2016; www.saints365.blogspot.com.
5. St. Francis de Sales, *Thy Will Be Done: Letters to Persons in the World* (Manchester, N.H.: Sophia Institute Press, 1995), p. 33.
6. *United States Catholic Catechism for Adults*, USCCB (Washington, D.C.: United States Conference of Catholic Bishops, 2012), p. 463.
7. Mother Teresa, *No Greater Love* (Novato, Calif.: New World Library, 2016), p. 9.
8. Laura Vanderkam, *What the Most Successful People Do Before Breakfast* (New York: Penguin Books Limited, 2013), p. 10.
9. Ibid., p. 11.
10. Ibid., p. 13.
11. Lisa Brenninkmeyer, *Walking with Purpose* (North Palm Beach, Fla.: Beacon Publishing, 2013), p. 24.
12. Matthew Kelly, *Rediscover Jesus* (North Palm Beach, Fla.: Beacon Publishing, 2015), p. 121.

13. Gwendolyn Bounds, "How Handwriting Trains the Brain," *The Wall Street Journal*, October 5, 2010; www.wsj.com.

14. Ibid.

15. Pam A. Mueller, Daniel M. Oppenheimer, "The Pen Is Mightier Than the Keyboard: Advantages of Longhand Over Laptop Note Taking," *Association for Psychological Science*, April 23, 2014.

16. St. Teresa of Avila, *The Way of Perfection*, translated by E. Allison Peers (London: Sheed and Ward, 1977), p. 114.

17. Matthew Kelly, *Resisting Happiness* (North Palm Beach, Fla.: Beacon Publishing, 2016), pp. 2–3.

18. Andrew Stanton, *Finding Nemo*, directed by Andrew Stanton and Lee Unkrich (Emeryville, Calif.: Disney/Pixar, 2003).

19. Pope Francis, Wednesday General Audience, May 25, 2016.

20. St. Teresa of Avila, *The Way of Perfection* (New York: Image Books, 1964), p. 80.

21. St. Teresa of Avila, *The Interior Castle* (Mineola, N.Y.: Dover Publications, Inc., 2007), chapter I.

22. St. Teresa of Avila, quoted by Dr. Tom Neal on the Word on Fire website; https://www.wordonfire.org/resources/blog/loving-god-unto-distraction-st-bernard-and-the-struggle-of-prayer/4895/.

23. Fulton Sheen, *Through the Year with Fulton Sheen* (San Francisco: Ignatius Press, 2003), p. 16.

24. http://www.usccb.org/prayer-and-worship/liturgy-of-the-hours/index.cfm.

25. Josemaría Escrivá, *The Way: The Essential Classic of Opus Dei's Founder* (New York: Image/Doubleday, 2006), p. 15.

26. Ann Voskamp Facebook post, 9/29/16.

27. Matthew Kelly, *Four Signs of a Dynamic Catholic* (North Palm Beach, Fla.: Beacon Publishing, 2012), p. 61.

28. There are variations of the Examen and tutorials on how to use this prayer available at http://www.ignatianspiri-tuality.com/ignatian-prayer/the-examen.

29. *The Annunciation*, by Henry Ossawa Tanner (1859–1937).

30. St. Alphonsus Liguori, *How to Converse with God* (Charlotte, N.C.: TAN Books, 2015), chapter 4.

31. Thérèse of Lisieux, *Simply Surrender: 30 Days with a Spiritual Teacher* (Notre Dame, Ind.: Ave Maria Press, 2008).

32. *The Beauties of St. Francis de Sales* (London: Longman and Co., 1829), p. 4.

33. Jose Luis Gonzalez-Balado, *Mother Teresa: In My Own Words* (Liguori, Mo.: Liguori Publications, 1997), p. 9.

34. Sarah Young, *Jesus Calling: Enjoying Peace in His Presence* (Nashville: Thomas Nelson, 2011), pp. xii-xiii.

35. Archbishop Fulton Sheen, *St. Thérèse: A Treasured Love Story* (Irving, Tex.: Basilica Press, 2007), p. 115.

36. Susan Conroy, *Mother Teresa's Lessons of Love and Secrets of Sanctity* (Huntington, Ind.: Our Sunday Visitor, 2003), p. 201.

37. Ibid, p. 85.

38. Common paraphrase of St. Catherine of Siena, from the original: "If you are what you ought to be, you will light a fire not only there but in all of Italy," quoted in Suzanne

Noffke, *The Letters of Catherine of Siena*, Volume 3 (Tempe, Ariz.: Arizona Center for Medieval and Renaissance Studies, 2007).

39. Homily of Pope Francis, Domus Sanctae Marthae, March 18, 2014.

40. Mother Teresa, *No Greater Love, Commemorative Edition* (Novato, Calif.: New World Library, 2001), pp. 71–72.

41. Raymond Arroyo, *Mother Angelica's Little Book of Life Lessons and Everyday Spirituality* (New York: Doubleday, 2007), p. 21.

42. St. Francis de Sales, *Set Your Heart Free: 30 Days with a Spiritual Teacher* (Notre Dame, Ind.: Ave Maria Press, 2008).

# About the Author

**Mary Beth Weisenburger** is a magazine editor, a family humor columnist, and an author, but her favorite form of writing is prayer journaling. Praying with a pen every morning for years dramatically strengthened her spiritual life, even drawing her back home to the Catholic Church in 2013 after several decades away. She previously worked in senior positions in the banking and healthcare industries and has taught at the college level. She's a member of St. Michael's church choir, loves to sing at big Catholic weddings, and has recently begun facilitating book studies and retreats for women. Mary Beth is the grateful wife (thirty years and counting) to Steve and the mom to two amazing adult children, Curtis and Erin (who is married to an equally amazing son-in-law, Damon). You can find more of Mary Beth's prayer journaling reflections on her blog: prayingwithapen.com.

# THE
# DYNAMIC CATHOLIC
## INSTITUTE

## [MISSION]

To re-energize the Catholic Church in America by developing world-class resources that inspire people to rediscover the genius of Catholicism.

## [VISION]

To be the innovative leader in the New Evangelization helping Catholics and their parishes become the-best-version-of-themselves.

**Join us in re-energizing the Catholic Church.**
*Become a Dynamic Catholic Ambassador today!*

DynamicCatholic.com
Be Bold. Be Catholic.®